A Rainbow Book

To Phillis and Skip.
With memories of yesteryear
Have fun reading!
With warmest greetings,
Si. John
Dec. 1994

Sir John's Diary

The Fun-Tome of the Opera

Sir John van Kesteren

Library of Congress Cataloging-in-Publication Data

Kesteren, John van.
   Sir John's diary : the fun-tome of the opera / Sir John van Kesteren.
     p.   cm.
   ISBN 1-56825-022-3
   1. Kesteren, John van. 2. Tenors (Singers)—Biography.
ML420.K37A3 1994
782.1'092--dc20
[B]   94-36843
                                                 CIP
                                                 MN

Sir John's Diary: The Fun-Tome of the Opera
by Sir John van Kesteren

ISBN 1-56825-022-3

Copyright © 1994 by Sir John van Kesteren

Rainbow Books, Inc.
P. O. Box 430
Highland City, FL 33846-0430
Telephone/Fax (813) 648-4420

All rights reserved. No parts of this book may be used or reproduced or transmitted in any form or by any means, electronic or mechanical (except as follows for photocopying) without written permission of the author. Permission for photocopying can be obtained for internal or personal use, the internal or personal use of specific clients, and for eductional use, by paying the appropriate fee to Copyright Clearance Center, 222 Rosewood Dr., Danvers, MA 01923, USA.

All photographs by John van Kesteren
Cover Photo: John van Kesteren in the title role of the opera *Platea*,
                by Jean Philippe Rameau

First edition, 1994

            Printed in the United States of America.

*For my all-encompassing wife Louise,
without whom life has no meaning for me.*

In this, his second book, the celebrated Dutch tenor John van Kesteren tells the story of a life full of variety, passion and devotion. In a humorous and often satirical way, he portrays his youth in his home country of The Netherlands, as well as the dramatic World War II years there, which he miraculously survives as a young resistance fighter.

As a multi-talented performing artist, he describes his studies in Paris and Vienna, and the professional vagaries of his life as an internationally recognized opera and concert singer. During his many travels around the world, he encounters many celebrities of all means and standing.

Referring to "Famous people who met me," he often portrays them on the world stage in an ironical, witty way, at that not sparing himself. Above all, however, he writes in an engagingly outspoken and amusing tone about the world around him in the often tragicomic realm of creativity.

Acknowledgments

Louise Rouner van Kesteren, for editing the initial copy.

Köszönöm to Laszlo Dosa for lending his intelligence and knowledge in re-editing and typesetting this book.

The *Jupiter Courier* for printing some of the original chapters, which created the interest.

Introduction

My wife Louise threatened me with culinary countermeasures, should I ever again dare to waste our time by writing another book. However, after having received moderately favorable press reviews for my first book, *Notitie's van een Notenkraker (Notes of a Notecracker)*, I felt as though I was flying on golden wings. Encouraged by the sympathetic reception, I managed to overcome my initial reluctance and began dreaming about a titanic reward with promises of immortality that was awaiting me in Stockholm — the Nobel Prize for *Illiteracy*.

After Alfred Nobel uncovered the formula $C_3\text{-}H_5(NO_3)_3$ which became the recipe for dynamite, he was seized with an explosive thought. Prompted by a moral streak in his character, he decided to appease his conscience with an act of unprecedented liberal generosity.

Every year since 1901, one *belletrist* from among other literary prize fighters is summoned to the Valhalla of Science in Sweden's capital to receive from the hands of the king a financial token of appreciation for being an outstanding genius in the circle of intellectual superiority.

For seven long, disappointing years, I waited in vain for the phone call from the land of the Vikings, but the king failed me. Could it possibly be that he never even read my book? Then one day, the cup of my endurance overflowed and I decided to take a second chance.

Ernest Hemingway, my great idol in the writing guild, had to wait 24 years for his reward from Stockholm. That inspired me to give birth to the motto, "If Hemingway can use his mind, my brain cells cannot stay behind." Among other honors, this literary giant was awarded the premier prize in literature for his book about an old Cuban fisherman and the sea in an unequaled emotional novel of understatement.

In retracing Hemingway's footsteps, I decided to go where this master of laconic dialogue had spent many laid-back days of his life. For my first trip to Key West, I took up my abode in a small lodging house, surrounded by tropical shrubs and lush palmetto trees. It was located just behind the partly overgrown Spanish colonial style house in Olivia Street, where the great writer had made his home on and off from 1927 until his untimely ending at his own hands in 1961.

Obviously longing for arcane excitement on the night of my arrival in Key West, I visited Sloppy Joe's, E. H.'s favorite bar in Duval Street, where he was a frequent guest, known as Erny, at the regular table of the boozing pundit. The table is still in place today, as is the chair where he greased his gills with his favorite Cuban rum. The greasing often ended in a bacchanalia, with E. H. picking up the tab for the entire guzzling crowd.

The mere idea of pressing my simplistic butt on the structure where once the cerebral posterior of the Great One had sat, should probably be enough for divine inspiration, I thought. Therefore, I ordered Erny's sugar cane juice and awaited the heavenly stimulus for creative activity.

After several refills and prayerful sighs, I came to the discouraging conclusion that I was probably sitting in the wrong chair, since nothing invigorated my thinking faculties. Deeply disconcerted, I left the cavernous tavern and knocked about the sparsely lit main street toward the small, picturesque harbor.

At the end of the street was an oysterbar with a rickety terrace that obviously had had to endure many a hurricane. It looked out over the waterway between Cuba and

Introduction xiii

the Keys, exposing majestic yachts and humble fishing hulks to wind and weather.

The tepidity of the night was heavily laden with the scent of tar and fish. I could imagine vividly how Papa Hemingway must have peered across the timeless horizon, recalling his productive years in nearby Havana. People had observed how he, absorbed in thought, beheld the skyline for a long period of time, as the scarlet evening Sun painted the approaching night.

I also looked intensely into the advancing nightfall, but my inspiration gave no sign of improvement. Dejected, I walked to my lodgings, passing by oleander and hibiscus gardens as the sweet smell of jasmine bushes made me dreamy. Without much difficulty, I slept the sleep of fatigue and the abundance of rum.

On the second day of my stay at the lodge, I discovered a pen and paper in the portfolio in my room. As at the time of the great wine feast given by King Belshazzar 2,425 years ago in Babylon, where an invisible hand wrote words of warning on the wall, there came to my amazement an impulse from on high, prompting me to take up the quill and begin my second literary opus.

In my aging operatic audacity, I would like to express my appreciation to the memory of Ernest Hemingway for having inspired "the old man and the high C." May Apollo in the heaven of the muses forgive my boldness.

Contents

Photographic Contents / 19

Chapter One —
 The boy who wanted to sing all evening / 21
Chapter Two —
 Waking up one day to an invasion / 25
Chapter Three —
 Surviving day-to-day amid war,
 hunger and the invaders / 29
Chapter Four —
 Strange silhouettes in a wartime nightmare / 33
Chapter Five —
 Encounter with the "Executioner" / 37
Chapter Six —
 To be or not to be in the
 Apeldoorn cemetery / 41
Chapter Seven —
 A scheme to kill the Nazi beast in Holland / 45
Chapter Eight —
 On a harrowing mission in Holland / 49
Chapter Nine —
 Music, molasses and
 pancakes bring brief truce / 55
Chapter Ten —
 Holland is finally liberated, but not
 before some parting atrocities / 61
Chapter Eleven —
 Fighting off starvation as war ends / 65

Chapter Twelve —
   What to do when the war has ended? / 69
Chapter Thirteen —
   A tenor joins the Royal Conservatory / 73
Chapter Fourteen —
   Learning to sing from the great masters / 79
Chapter Fifteen —
   Madame Boulanger and *La vie Parisienne* / 85
Chapter Sixteen —
   Surviving the opening
   night's monkey business / 91
Chapter Seventeen —
   A shaky audition, and then the wait / 97

Photographic Section
   (see Photographic Contents) / 103

Chapter Eighteen —
   An untimely and a timely entrance
   to the opera *Don Giovanni* / 125
Chapter Nineteen —
   How the beautiful, nearsighted
   singer made my day / 131
Chapter Twenty —
   The teenage opera groupie who
   stalked my every move / 137
Chapter Twenty-One —
   What did we ever do before television? / 145
Chapter Twenty-Two —
   With Clark, Lana, Victor and Lex
   on location in Delft / 149
Chapter Twenty-Three —
   Tales of weak bladder, strong voice / 157
Chapter Twenty-Four —
   The spirit of the dead composer played on / 161
Chapter Twenty-Five —
   My surprise singing partner before the DAR / 167

Contents

Chapter Twenty-Six —
    Herbert, The Great / 173
Chapter Twenty-Seven —
    Ill fortune seldom comes alone / 177
Chapter Twenty-Eight —
    What secrets lay in the message
    from Andrei Gromyko? / 183
Chapter Twenty-Nine —
    Despite my agony, the show went on / 191
Chapter Thirty —
    Shortcuts don't pay / 199
Chapter Thirty-One —
    From Chaos to Man / 203
Chapter Thirty-Two —
    I couldn't stop thinking about
    that lovely girl in blue / 207
Chapter Thirty-Three —
    An emotional decision / 211
Chapter Thirty-Four —
    It's a tough life / 217

About the author / 221

Help the Hungry at Home / 225

Photographic Contents

Page 103 — (top) When John was still "Little Johnny" — with father, mother and brother, Cor, sporting a crew cut.
(bottom) John, brother, Cor, and their dog, Wotan.

Page 104 — (top) John, little sister, Greetje, and their late brother, Cor.
(bottom left) My very first tuxedo, at age 20.
(bottom right) Posing for a role in the Metro-Goldwyn movie, *Betrayed*. I made it!

Page 105 — My very first leading role as "Marquis" in the French Opera, *Les Cloches de Corneville*, 1943.

Page 106 — Still singing, 50 years later in 1993, as the "Messenger" in *Aida*.

Page 107 — In the startling production of the *Fledemaus*, as "Prince Orlofsky," at the Amsterdam Opera House.

Page 108 — (top) In the title role as "the Count of Ory," in Rossini's opera of the same name, at the Berlin Opera House.
(bottom) With the legendary Tito Gobbi, in Verdi's *Falstaff*, at the Cologne Opera House.

Page 109 — (top) As "Prince Sou-Chong" in Lehar's *Land of Smiles* during a television production in Vienna.
(bottom) Recording for Deutsche Grammophone of the *Opera Palestrina*, with Swedish colleague, Nicolai Gedda.

Page 110 — (top) With Bayreuth basses, Bernt Weikl and Walter Berry, during a television session in London.
(bottom) With star soprano and friend Kiri Te Kanawa, at London's Sheperton Film Studio, shooting *Figaro*.

Page 111 — (top) Recording *Carmina Burana* for E.M.I., with Conductor Riccardo Muti and Composer Carl Orff.
(bottom) Eurovision television show in Amsterdam. The late Josephine Baker in conversation with Queen Beatrix, while I am telling the latest Joke to Prince Claus of the Netherlands.

Page 112 — (top) Paying a visit to a vocal colleague from the other guild — Tony Bennett.
(bottom) The night I was knighted by the hand of the Ambassador of the Netherlands.

Page 113 — (top) As "Basilio" in *Le Nozze Di Figaro*, at the Salzburg Festival, with Graziella Scutti and Dietrich Fischer-Dieskau.
(bottom) Recording session in Vienna with friend and colleague, Hermann Prey.
Page 114 — (top) With star conductor Raphael Kubilik, during a concert tour in Switzerland.
(bottom) Louise and I flank our legendary singing teacher, Vera Schwarz, who sang the world premier of *Land of Smiles* with Richard Tauber.
Page 115 — As the "Prompter" in Richard Strauss's *Capriccio*, at the Brussels Opera House.
Page 116 — (top) Louise likes it! Vocalizing at the concert hall in Barcelona.
(bottom) As "Nureddin" in *The Barber of Bagdad*, by Peter Cornelius, at the (then) East-Berlin Opera House.
Page 117 — (top) Meeting Queen Elisabeth of Belgium after my concert in Brussels.
(bottom) With lovely Loni Andersen during a night on the town.
Page 118 — (top) Concert at "La Scala" in Milano, with Zubin Metha as conductor.
(bottom) Shooting the movie, *Carmina Burana*, at the Bavaria Studio in Munich, with friend — and one of the greatest composers of this century — Carl Orff.
Page 119 — (top) As "Zephoris" in Adam's lyric opera, *si j'etais Roi* (King for a Day), at the Munich Opera House.
(bottom) As "Marquis de Chateauneuf" in *Zar and Zimmerman* (Czar and Carpenter) at the Vienna Opera House.
Page 120 — In the role that gave me so much trouble, as "Harlequin" in Wolf-Ferrari *Le Donne Curiose* (The Inquisitive Women).
Page 121 — (top) With Louise at our winter home in Munich.
(bottom) With Louise and Sandy in our tulip garden in Munich.
Page 122 — In performance for "Help the Hungry at Home, Inc."
Page 123 — (top) John and volunteers buy, box and deliver food for the needy on a regular basis.
(bottom) Appreciative recipients receiving food boxes . . .
Page 124 — The greatest day of my life. Louise has just said, "Yes!"

Chapter One

The boy who wanted to sing all evening

I must have been about four years old when the proper young "Miss" at the kindergarten where I "studied" *put up and shut up*, had the brilliant inspiration of asking me to sing "second voice" during our daily sing-song hour. Although I did not know that one could have a "second voice," I managed, to her great satisfaction, to fulfill her wish.

In my innocent youth, I displayed a natural talent for music that would have made Wolfgang Amadeus pale with envy. The "Miss" was proud as a peacock in Bellingrath's Gardens to have made such a find in the thrift shop of infant talent. It was, for her and for me, the beginning of a new life after four years of blissful ignorance.

We had at home, in those years, a shiny, black-lacquered upright piano in the so-called Sunday parlor. And from that happy moment on, the "Miss" (whose real name was Small, but whom my father later renamed Miss Great) often came to our home to teach me the rudiments of music.

Singing was so much a part of my daily existence that my parents often had to resort to all sorts of persuasion to keep me from singing into the night after I already had been between the sheets for several hours. That was my first encounter with sheet music!

After 36 verses of *Twinkle, Twinkle, Little Star*, my parents could curb my aptitude for improvisation only by promising me that the next day also had 24 hours for singing opportunities. Thumb in mouth, I fell asleep, dreaming of endless galaxies filled with radiant stars.

Four years before all of this took place, I was born in the City of International Justice, namely The Hague (or

The Hedge, in English) in The Netherlands as the middle offspring of three contributions toward our posterity. I was the second son of State Police Inspector Hendrick van Kesteren and his wife, Gerrie Vreedeveld.

Kesteren is a town of about 16,000 inhabitants in the eastern part of Holland. The word *van* means *from*, so consequently, van Kesteren means *from* Kesteren, such as Vanderbilt means from the Bilt, a town of some 11,000 people. My mother's maiden name, Vreedeveld, translates into English as Peace Field — and a world of peace she was!

It was a stroke of unforeseeable destiny that massive unemployment at the end of the 19th century forced my father, a young whippersnapper of 12 springs old, to leave the country of his birth. My grandfather, who was a weaver, took his entire family of seven, his scanty belongings and adventuresome spirit, and walked for four days eastward into the neighboring Rhineland of Germany where many weaving mills were to be found at that time.

Every goldmark was welcome to the young family, so 12-year-old Hendrick spent 12 hours daily at the weaving loom, returning home at night like a worn-out bundle of misery, with his earnings of two marks held in his little fist. There were no unions at the time which would have protected children from work abuse.

My mother's family was no more fortunate in procuring employment. Her family of eight also crossed the border into the realm of Kaiser Wilhelm who wielded the scepter in pre-World War I Germany and who later, as destiny would have it, was forced to flee to Holland where he later died and was buried as an exile.

An interest in singing encouraged my parents to join one of the many choirs of the Rhineland and it was through this love of music that they developed an interest in each other. According to the custom of those good old days, they became engaged and subsequently married. They packed their belongings into knapsacks and returned westward, home to the land of milk and cheese, wooden shoes and tulip bulbs. There they lived happily together for 52 years. The State Police in The Hague was looking for reinforcements and clean-looking, healthy Dutchmen 21 years old or older could apply. Thus my father traveled to the "big city," strained his brain cells in several exams and was shortly thereafter named a "lucky winner." It was then that the time was ripe for a turn to prosperity and, lo and behold, I was born! Although I was not allotted many earthly goods in my cot, a providential future had begun for me.

Chapter Two

Waking up one day to an invasion

To tell you that my father was drafted as a cavalryman in Holland during World War I, and that he had a powerful tenor voice and a huge mustache with turned-up ends and big, black, fiery eyes, might not be of any interest to the reader.

That I was given a Doberman pincher on my 10th birthday, who turned blind after one year, and that I, some years later, took up studies in electronics, are also bits of information of little significance.

However, it may be of greater interest that I voluntarily signed up for six years of navy service on the aircraft carrier *Karel Doorman* at the naive age of 17 springs, which was almost fatal for me.

The *Doorman* would be leaving for the Dutch East Indies and that fact alone sharpened my hunger for life and doubled the beat of my adventurous heart. Alas, six months after signing up, I was dropped like a sack of cement by our admiralty due to a total lack of military discipline.

This was a providential act of fate because some years later, in 1942, after World War II had started, the *Doorman* and its crew went down in the warm but roaring waves of the Java Sea, fighting a five-times-superior Japanese fleet. No one survived!

I am still grateful for my forced discharge. It is better to be alive in sunny Florida than to be at the bottom of the Java Sea. Moreover, since 1948, that area is no longer a colony of The Netherlands.

After returning to the parental nest, I first found a job as an electrical technical designer for cinemas, When I discovered that the owner of the small firm in which I was employed was an active member of the Communist Party. trying to convince me that the doctrine of Karl Marx had more sugar on the cake than I was willing to believe, I had seen enough.

Luckily, my father found me a job of a lifetime, complete with retirement and everything else that a civil servant with the Dutch Post and Telegraph Service could ask for.

My job was to promote efficiency in telecommunications, and I stayed with the governmental "club" for 11 years! During the difficult war years, I was able to contribute to the defeat of the enemy by drawing up plans for a radio transmitter station for the German military machine in such a manner that no one would notice that the thing was sabotaged to blow up into little pieces when put into use.

On the morning of May 10, 1940, we had intended to sleep long because my little sister had her birthday the day before and the celebration went on into the early morning hours. However, my brother who slept in the same room with me, woke me up with the information that huge, black and slow-moving airplanes with "Greek crosses" painted on their wings and tail, were literally hanging over our house. It was 5 o'clock in the morning!

First I thought that it was one of his practical jokes that often amused our family, but when my father turned on the radio to find out the meaning of this strange aviational phenomenon, we really woke up. Without laughing.

The newscaster announced that an incredulously dastardly act of war was being committed against Holland by her neighbors to the east, the Germans. They had invaded the small peace-loving country of the wooden shoes, tulip fields and windmills. My country!

The scoundrels ruined, bombed and starved our nation during the next years. They made our people into slaves and killed or put into concentration camps everyone who said or showed that he or she was not in agreement with the new mental and physical torture the occupiers introduced. Five years of Nazi barbarism had began for the Dutch.

Chapter Three

Surviving day-to-day amid war, hunger and the invaders

It might seem a contradiction but even during the years of Nazi occupation in Holland, there were pleasant moments. For instance, one could still be a Catholic or a communist, or member of the Dutch Reformed Church. Priests, ministers, football players and referees, homosexuals, fortunetellers and swindlers, as well as dissidents of all sorts were all in the same boat where occupation, tyranny and plundering reigned.

There was much praying and talking because every day could bring a forced farewell from home, friends, family and even life. No time was wasted with the question of what car to buy or use next, because the Nazis had seized 90 percent of the gasoline supply.

For strategic reasons, the Germans had removed all the road signs, and when a Dutch civilian was asked by a German convoy leader for the shortest route to Rotterdam or Amsterdam, it gave one a feeling of great satisfaction to be able to send the enemy the wrong way. It was one of the few ways for the man in the street to contribute to final victory.

For a man, the daily thoughts were first, how to avoid being picked up and sent to a labor camp, transported in railroad cars like cattle to the slaughterhouse. With practically no food in the industrialized part of Western Holland, the only daily thought of the woman was, "What can I put on the plates tonight?" Even the oldest and most distinguished people walked in the woods to collect small twigs of wood, because cutting down a tree was "honored" with capital punishment.

On potbellied stoves at home, the wives prepared meals of tulip bulbs or sugar beets which tasted so flat that today a cow would shrug her udder at it.

The finely-cut fiber of the sugar beets and other stinking components were rolled into pieces of newspaper in order to smoke them as cigarettes. Doctors warned not to smoke the rubbish, should one wish to live to see the end of the war. On the black market, one could buy real cigarettes for $85 to $100 a pack.

During the cold winter of 1944, all foods were confiscated by the Nazis and sent over the border to the "Thousand-Year Empire." The ration-coupon books wore out in our empty wallets because of the "No Merchandise" sign displayed on most of the store windows.

Just before I was to leave my hometown of The Hague to go into hiding, I left the city with a friend to find food at some farmers located in the middle of the country.

Money had no value for people anymore, so I took three brand new bed sheets to barter. My friend and I had bicycles that had seen better years and, for lack of rubber tires, our wheels were rimmed with wooden "tires."

A farmer exchanged my sheets for 20 kilos of life-saving potatoes which I put in a pillowcase and draped with care around the handlebars. This, however, meant that we had to walk the rest of the journey. After my friend had traded in his grandfather's gold watch for 15 kilos of rye flour, we trekked the 150 miles homeward, traveling along country roads, to avoid the big cities and military checkpoints.

We walked for four days until I became so tired and undernourished that I suddenly collapsed and my friend had to carry me to a small café along the roadside. The innkeeper made us some porridge and let us sleep for several hours on a billiard table where we dreamt the dreams of forget and forgive.

However cruel, we were abruptly awakened by the innkeeper with the alarming news that a German truck had

Surviving day-to-day amid war, hunger and the invaders

just stopped in front of the café. Our eyes were hardly opened when three Germans entered the dimly lit room. Two of them were in uniform and the third man was dressed in a Bavarian-looking coat and hat, complete with feather. Their piercing *Heil Hitler!* immediately poisoned the atmosphere. With dangling legs, we continued to sit on sleepily on the billiard table, too paralyzed to move.

"I said *Heil Hitler!*" the Bavarian said sarcastically. His face, adorned with rimless John Denver glasses, resembled more and more the late Erich von Stroheim.

"Yes sir!" was all we could bring forward, while we jumped off the table, not prepared for patriotic heroism.

For five seconds, there was silence but suddenly he opened his coat and a revolver appeared in his hand.

"Repeat *Heil Hitler!* 500 times! Now!" he shouted at us. I was petrified and could not say a word. Slowly, the Bavarian raised his gun and put it to my temple, like a butcher does with a cow in the slaughterhouse.

"He will shoot, if you don't cooperate," whispered one of the soldiers just inches from my face.

I don't know how many of those pointless greetings I had rattled off, when the Bavarian dropped his gun and punched me violently in the eyes and nose. My blood immediately began flowing and soiled even further my already dirty shirt.

While they were laughing and drinking, we continued our German greeting.

Eventually, without paying for their bill, the Germans walked to the door, once more administering excruciating kicks to our lower abdomen as they were passing us by.

Arriving at the door, the Bavarian turned around and said, *Was ist das?* pointing to our bicycles and foodstuff.

"It belongs to them," said the innkeeper.

"Wrong," said the German, "it belongs to us." And without further ado, he picked up the bicycles and life-saving potatoes and flour. They were never to be seen again.

Three days later, we arrived home empty-handed and

deadly tired, but happy to see our relatives in spite of the hunger, pain and misery. I was not able to save my father from physical suffering, due to lack of life-saving nourishment. This resulted in the almost unbearable pain of bone cancer of which he consequently died some years later. The food stolen by the Nazis might have saved his life.

Chapter Four

Strange silhouettes in a wartime nightmare

At the end of 1944, the Germans — seeing the end of the "Thousand-Year Empire" drawing near after only 11 years — became more nervous every day, and thus more dangerous.

Young men of my age at that time were in great demand by the Nazis, to be picked off the streets and sent to the *Reich* for forced labor, so the Germans could send their own men to the front in far-off Russia.

To escape the claws of the enemy, I decided to go into hiding in a small town called Apeldoorn, 60 miles from the border between Holland and Germany. I stayed there until the town was liberated by Canadian troops in May 1945.

Entertainment did not amount to much in the Apeldoorn of 1944. The curfew required the residents to stay home between 8 p.m. and 6 a.m.

Since there was no electricity anymore anyway and reading was impossible without light, most people went to bed early, as there was little else to do at night. However, Apeldoorn had an operetta society, a good conductor, some lovely sopranos and I had a singing voice.

One of the lovely sopranos caught my eye. Not only was she lovely, but she also was a fine pianist who could help me study my roles. I discovered that in the lovely soprano's house, there was an empty room, just large enough to house a young, ambitious tenor eager to study as many roles as possible.

Her father, a white-haired six-foot-seven-inch-tall man who was a member of the constabulary, also was in the Dutch underground movement. Approximately 3,000 people in Holland were in resistance groups during the war years. They lived very dangerously because they were tortured or shot on the spot by the Germans if caught in action.

My soprano's father was arrested at 3 o'clock in the morning on a moonless night while picking up arms and ammunition that had been dropped by British glider pilots. The Germans had been informed by a collaborator and my girlfriend's father was sent to a German concentration camp where he was later shot like a rabbit. No mercy.

After he had left home, his wife decided that it would be improper for me to continue my stay there and, with the help of a friend, I moved to a large brownstone house in the center of town. The house was fine, but it was directly next door to the main office of the Gestapo headquarters, as I found out a day later. But by sitting on a whale's back, one can follow his actions, so I decided to stay.

I moved in with a family of four, who had two sons in their teens. The father, who was an engineer, put me up in a tiny room under the eaves of the attic with only a bed and one chair, but small hearts have small desires.

The third night of my stay was a very cold winter night and I got up at 3 a.m. to get my overcoat to use it as an additional blanket. While I looked through the small window that gave a view of the moonlit street below, I heard whispering, so close to my ear that I thought someone was standing behind me.

I turned around but there was no one there.

My breath failed me as I again heard that whispering voice.

I was not alone!

The eaves of the attic had on both sides a slanting wooden wall and when I slid my hand along the paneled wall, one section moved backward. I pushed a little harder and as I put my head into the opening that was created, I saw a small room in the darkness of the night.

In the rear of the long but very narrow space was another small window, also with a view of the street below.

Strange silhouettes in a wartime nightmare

My blood stopped circulating because, silhouetted against the light were two motionless figures standing in front of the window.

With a trembling voice, I asked, "Is someone there?"

A silly question in the situation, but nothing else came to mind to break the silence. However, there was no answer.

This was too much for me. Hastily, I let the panel go, which closed by itself. Shivery and shaky from the experience and the cold, I slipped back into my bed and pulled the thin sheet up over my head as if to protect myself. I could not sleep again that night.

When the first ray of light sneaked through the little window of my attic room, I got up to go down for breakfast. Passing the place where I knew there was a secret door, I felt like Norman Bates in *Psycho*, but that was only a movie.

Sliding my hand over the cold wood, I didn't find any indication of an opening and, for a moment, thought that all had been just a nightmare. At the breakfast table, I told about my strange experience that night.

The master of the house stopped me in my tracks and took me by my arm into the kitchen. There, with a soft voice, he told me that for the past four years he had been hiding three Jewish men under the eaves of the attic. If the German Secret Service, which regularly went on house-searching raids, should discover the Jews, they would not only be sent to the gas chambers of Dachau or Bergen-Belsen, but the family who risked their lives by hiding them would be executed on the spot.

To me, those unselfish people are the real heroes of World War II.

Chapter Five

Encounter with the "Executioner"

Until the end of World War II, I stayed in hiding in the same house, next to the Gestapo headquarters, in that small city, Apeldoorn, in the center of Holland. After I had told my landlord, Mr. Driels, about my scary discovery in the attic of his villa, he knew there was a dilemma.
Was I a traitor or a patriot?
To test me, he sent me, under a pretext, on irregular trips in and around town, with small packages that I had to leave at certain addresses. He did not tell me the contents, but one night the curiosity became too much and I opened one of the packages that he had given me.
To my astonishment, I discovered these packages contained ration cards, a familiar commodity in those days.
However, the cards were reserved for Jewish people who were in hiding. Involuntarily and unknowingly, I was working for the Dutch underground movement and became aware of its activities.
I told Mr. Driels about my impudence and although I gave him a fright, he was glad that the burden of uncertainty of me being "good" or "bad" was now off his shoulders.
However, it was all just the beginning for me because, having said "A," I was forced to go all the way to "Z" as well.
For some time, I had delivered ration cards that for some people brought life through food, but for others brought death if they were caught by the Germans.
After seven weeks, Mr. Driels stopped my risky job before somebody became suspicious. Getting another job in those days was as easy as digging a hole, so next I

became a Forest Police Officer.

I was given a forged identity card with a false name, a broad white armband and a uniform cap with the legend, "Forest Police." The armband did not raise my status a bit but the cap made me look as important as a general or, if you wish, a hotel doorman. I looked like someone who could be somebody!

My official duty was to see that no wood was stolen or trees chopped down on a certain property of the crown. In peacetime, it had been the residence of Queen Wilhelmina, but from 1941 on, the chief representative of the German *Reich* in The Netherlands, Herr Seyss-Inquart, had set up housekeeping there by simply confiscating the majestic palace.

My instruction from the underground movement was to shadow the "Executioner of Holland" during his daily outings in the forests around Arnhem.

Frequently, riding on his gray horse, he crossed our path, unaware of the fact that my partner and I, pretending to be Forest Police officers, reported to our leaders soon afterward our observations about the time, place and number and rank of the people in his company.

Through this system, the movements of the most notorious and dreaded man in The Netherlands were known at all times.

One morning when dew and fog were still hanging in the silent forest, we heard the squeaking sound of a saw cutting wood. After some searching, we discovered a little old lady trying to cut down a huge birch tree with a small hand saw.

When we told her that this was against the law, tears like thick pearls trickled down her pale cheeks. She mumbled that her house was ice-cold and that there was no firewood left in the cellar anymore. That her husband was confined to bed, and, and, and...

We looked with pity at the bundle of misery that stood in front of us and decided to take action. "You stay here,

Encounter with the "Executioner"

I'll be back in 15 minutes," I promised my partner. Soon I was back with a big saw, and we started our wearisome job.

We worked as if we were out to win first prize in a wood cutting contest, but also like burglars who knew the family might come home at any minute. To the little woman we gave an order to stand guard down the pathway and look for any danger that may be in sight.

Before long, the felled 24-foot tree lay dead as a fallen giant at our feet and we started to chop it into transportable pieces.

Barely had we the first sections behind us when "Grandma" came running with a terrified face and told us, quite out of breath, that two horses were coming down the pathway, with two men in uniform sitting on their backs.

Oh, disastrous destiny, it was Seyss-Inquart, the butcher, and his adjutant, on their morning ride. "What is going on here?" he wanted to know.

I told him that, as he could see on our uniform caps, we were members of the Forest Police and that we had caught the woman in the act of stealing wood, and that we were going to arrest her and see to it that she would be punished.

What I said was so nauseating that we could have vomited instantly, but it was the only way to get her and us out of trouble.

Seyss-Inquart looked from his high horse through his thick eyeglasses down to the broken figure at his feet.

"Where do you live?" he asked the lady in a soft voice, but she was so scared and horror-stricken that she only could look at him through the flood of tears in her eyes. Now Seyss-Inquart looked at me and I thought I saw hostility in his face.

"Why don't you just let the lady go?" he snarled at me. "It could happen to your own mother," and with a short "Come!" to his adjutant, he turned his horse and continued his ride.

Our muscles relaxed and we could breathe normally

again. The lady only understood my Quisling-like behavior after we had gone down to the forestry where we borrowed a cart, loaded the wood unto it and drove it to the woman's home where we felt like Help the Hungry at Home workers.

We did not report about our experiences with Seyss-Inquart. The incident demonstrated the complexity of his Dr. Jekyll and Mr. Hyde personality where good and bad could be in one body.

After the war, along with most of his fellow war criminals, Seyss-Inquart was tried in Nuremberg and hanged in 1948.

Chapter Six

To be or not to be
in the Apeldoorn cemetery

While Holland was crushed under the iron boot of Nazism, I left my beloved hometown of The Hague to take up hiding in a small town called Apeldoorn, in the eastern part of the country.

Ironically, the fact that Andrew Carnegie in 1913 had pampered The Hague with the present of the Peace Palace that, at this moment, houses the International Court of Justice, did not impress the Germans. Instead of pursuing Peace and Justice, they ruled with War and Tyranny.

On a bleak, rainy day in November 1943, Apeldoorn and the street where I lived were raided once again. All the men between the ages of 18 and 60 were ordered to be out in front of their homes by 5 a.m. the next morning to be assembled like a herd of cows about to be milked.

Special trains transported the men to the *Gross Deutsches Reich*, the Great German Empire, from whence only a few would return alive.

There was a dilemma!

My landlord at that time, who was not blessed with a golden character, hit upon the idea of crawling up through a hidden trapdoor into the attic of his house, where we would surely not be discovered by the hunters.

My brother had used the same method successfully in The Hague a year before. Having escaped from forced labor in Germany, he went into hiding for three months under the floorboards of the kitchen in my parents' home.

That space was only three feet high and filled with dirt and vermin but, to save his skin, he lived on a mattress in complete darkness because there was no electricity anymore in The Hague. However, SS troops who rounded up the men started to empty their rifles into the floors, forcing the stowaways into daylight.

With this knowledge in mind, my landlord and I opened the trapdoor to the attic which emitted a musty smell of moisture and old books, that penetrated our nostrils.

"I'll go first," said my landlord whose 230 pounds had accumulated mainly around his middle and his belly. I pushed and pulled to get him through the small hole, but the spare tire around his waist did not prove to be a safety belt for him.

"I can't get through it," he lamented with emotion and, for one moment, I was sorry for him. But then, suddenly, in a quarrelsome tone as if he was speaking to his wife: "But you're not going to go up there either! Both of us or neither of us." And with a thump, he pulled shut my gateway to safety.

So that was that! What now?

He weighed some 90 pounds more on the scales than I did. Therefore, it didn't seem advisable to me to try and change his intentions with my fist. However, mindful of Shakespeare's wisdom, I concluded that the question was — *to be or not to be!?*

There was not much time left for me to brainstorm for the solution to the problem. A few hundred yards from the landlord's house there was a graveyard, surrounded by a seven-foot-high wall, and in seconds, I decided to take up my hiding place there.

Without any further ado, I dashed to the wall and climbed over it, dropping down onto the graveyard grounds below. I was enveloped immediately with a silent, depressing forlornness seeping through the chilly November night.

Should I be caught and shot on sight, at least I was in the right place to find my final rest. After some groping around, I discovered a lovely, large, somewhat leaning tombstone, with a family's inscriptions carved into it.

This monument and the family of four buried beneath

it in the year of our Lord 1892, saved my night. Ducked away behind the granite hiding place, I felt like Boris Karloff in *Bride of Frankenstein*.

I sat there, hour-upon-hour, while from far off, I could hear the shouting voices of the SS hunters, piercing my soul to the very marrow of my bones. Should they enter the cemetery, I would be facing a very bitter future.

A full moon shone hypocritically through the leafless trees and played hide-and-seek with the clouds and, intermittently, with me. Suddenly, what normally would be a curse was, in my situation, a blessing.

A stealthy, typical November fog rolled out over the tombstones, looking like a downy blanket of anesthetized white foam. I tried to remain completely still and did not dare to stir because I could hear the shouting voices coming closer every minute. What goes through one's mind in such a situation is difficult to put into words.

Loneliness, fear, the biting cold and general misery do not make it possible to have a normal train of thought. One is terribly alone and the only way to find relief is to pray. However, promises made in desperation are long forgotten one week later.

Mankind is an insipid creature.

I had left the landlord's house in great haste, forgetting food or warm clothing. Consequently, I was frozen stiff and had caught the cold of a lifetime.

Finally, I was able to leave the protection of "Tombstone City" as the gray of morning announced a day that was considerably fresher than I was.

Lethargically, I climbed the wall once more, in reverse order. Tiptoeing through the empty street so as not to awake sleeping dogs, I approached my boarding house and rang the doorbell.

The shrill sound of the bell penetrated the stillness of the young morning but there was no answer to my impatient appeal. Thinking that my landlord had been picked up during the raid, I felt ashamed of my thoughts and "wishes" of the previous night — wishing the rascal so many inconveniences that he could have filled three lives with the pain of it.

Not knowing where to go next, I sat for several hours on the doorsteps of the house, like a desperate dog waiting for his master to take him on the daily walk.

Just as sleep started to overpower my fatigued body, the door suddenly opened behind me and there, with a nauseating sneer on his pumpkin-like face, stood the landlord.

Having ransomed himself free by means of several 100 guilder notes, he had not been picked up by the SS butchers. I was so disgusted by the man's behavior that, without saying one word, I rushed upstairs, threw my sparse belongings into my paper maché suitcase and, with abhorrence, left hurriedly the place where I had lived for almost a year.

To find another boarding house in those years was almost as impossible as to buy an egg, so I was forced to walk for two days and two nights with my heart, soul and paper maché suitcase under my arm. At night, I slept on a park bench and covered myself with newspapers.

Finally, on the morning of the third day, I met an acquaintance who suggested an address where I might be able to stay. It had been a narrow escape and my prayers were answered, but I will not go willingly to a cemetery any more, as long as I live.

Chapter Seven

A scheme to kill the
Nazi beast in Holland

It was 1944 and the Nazis still occupied my home country, The Netherlands. I had unwittingly joined Section Apeldoorn of the resistance movement. My assignment was to distribute several harmless-looking pamphlets, as well as to deliver ration cards for Jews in hiding.

Since I obviously had not been observed or shot by the Gestapo, in spite of my tall, 6-foot-2-inch blond frame, I did catch the eye of my resistance superiors, whom I knew only by their undercover names. I was given the name Gerrit which, by the way, is one of my real names, and I was selected for more significant assignments.

That the job consequently was more hazardous did not bother the young, reckless lad, whose parental guidance in The Hague was some 200 miles away. I had only one goal and the end justified the means. I was determined that my country's good shall be my constant aim!

With few exceptions, all men and women who were selected for more perilous jobs were unmarried, so as not to make an eventual failure of a mission more painful to the relatives. We were trained by skilled men who did know how to use a gun and dynamite and did know how to knock someone out temporarily or for eternity.

After having distributed forged ration cards for three months to Jews in hiding, who could survive only by means of these little faked coupon books, and after having served as a Forest Policeman in the woods around Apeldoorn, observing the "hangman" Seyss-Inquart, the top Nazi in Holland, there was a new challenge in the making for me.

In those years, there were a great number of Barbies

and Demjanjuks in the concentration camps in The Netherlands, occupied with torture and killings. However, one of them was unsurpassed in bestiality. His name was Heinrich Rauter.

Born in 1895 in Berlin, he headed the Gestapo in Holland and was responsible for the execution of Dutch hostages and for the transportation of Dutch Jewish citizens to the gas chambers of Dachau and Auschwitz.

As a retribution for the killing of two German officers in Amsterdam, he gave orders to burn down 310 houses in the little town of Putten. Twelve-hundred men from Putten were picked up off the streets and were executed by a shot in the neck, after first having to dig their own graves.

Born out of a poor worker's family, the power-passioned Satan had put up his headquarters just outside of Apeldoorn in a side wing of the majestic palace of Queen Wilhelmina who had found temporary refuge in England two days before the German armies invaded The Netherlands in 1940.

The queen, by the way, spoke to her countrymen from London via BBC shortwave radio every night for full five years of the war. To be caught listening to the broadcast was punishable with transportation to a concentration camp.

Rauter's name was synonymous with terror, murder and fear, and it was decided by London Headquarters that he had to be put out of action. Since the royal palace was close to the city, Section Apeldoorn was selected to execute the plan to kill Rauter.

Not far from Arnhem, there was an old renovated farmhouse hidden in the woods, carrying the name De' Woeste Hoeve (The Gloomy Inn). Rauter was a frequent visitor there and it was planned to eliminate him during one of his visits. Hopefully, Holland would finally be freed of this inhuman creature.

My assignment in the conspiracy was to have myself

hired by a local gasoline station that was frequented by Rauter's and other Gestapo cars. The owner was a Dutch collaborator of the type that would turn in his blind grandmother if he could achieve favor with the Nazis.

Since gasoline was, at the time, reserved for military units at the front, it was strictly rationed and available only for extremely urgent missions in the occupied countries. German army engineers, therefore, had constructed cars that ran on wood-burners. Primarily using the trunk of a car, they had created a "furnace" that was stoked with matchbox-sized wooden blocks. By means of an additional water tank, a steam engine was created. This contraption would make all the struggles for oil unnecessary in our time because the cars drove just as well on steam as with gasoline and, moreover, without polluting the countryside.

It became my daily work to chop the wood into small pieces and prepare and dry them over a glowing oven. My instructions from the underground were to question the drivers of the frequently high-ranking Nazi officers about their destination, so I could provide them with enough wooden "fuel" for their burner.

I coded and forwarded to Section Apeldoorn this information, as well as the license plate number of the cars and the rank and number of military personnel. The Section now had an overall picture based on my daily observations and was eventually able to take measures to hurt the enemy.

In spite of three weeks of thorough preparation, unforeseeable complications thwarted the mission to do away with Rauter and he escaped unharmed. Rumor had it for several years after the war that the plot had been betrayed by a spy in the Section Apeldoorn, because an unusually high number of army personnel were in the Gloomy Inn that day. The four men who were to execute the mission were caught and hanged the next day.

In 1947 when I had just started to be paid for my singing, I was sent by my agent to give concerts in camps where political delinquents were detained.

One day, I had to perform at a camp just outside my hometown, The Hague. I could hardly believe my eyes when I entered the auditorium for, just in the middle of the first row, between two armed prison guards, sat Rauter.

Seeing in front of me the man who had during the war years ruthlessly ruled over life and death in Holland, made me reticent to perform. Fifty-thousand people died by his signature without given a chance to defend themselves.

Comprehending the significance of the moment, I asked for permission after the concert to speak with the prisoner and my wish was granted.

A wiry man stood straight as an arrow in front of me. A dueling scar decorated his sallow cheek as if flesh-marked by the beast. After long moments of silence, I started to talk about my weeks at the gasoline station in Apeldoorn and about my participation in the attempt at the Gloomy Inn.

Pride and arrogance reflected his character from the transparent blue eyes. Without any sign of understanding, he stared back at me, but he no longer could use his stare of daggers to his own advantage. The days of wine and roses, torture and murder had gone by forever, and his exit was dawning on the horizons.

Two weeks later, Rauter was hanged till he died.

Chapter Eight

On a harrowing mission in Holland

From August 1942 onward, the German Sixth Army launched a murderous offensive on the old fortress city of Stalingrad. In February 1943, its commander-in-chief, Field Marshal Paulus, refused to sacrifice 300,000 lives to the war god Mars and wisely surrendered the last battle, handing a major victory to the Russians.

After that disastrous defeat, the German eastern front began to crumble and gradually retreated westward.

Consequently, with each new day, the German army became more and more nervous in the occupied countries. This led to increased terror against the subjugated people. In Holland, this required the underground movement to expend ever greater efforts to counter the actions of the Nazis.

German engineers had constructed a counter-espionage radio station on one of the southwest islands of the Dutch province of Zeeland. This station could intercept and analyze coded messages broadcast to the underground movements on the mainland of Western Europe.

By intercepting messages to the underground, the German forces became increasingly effective in crushing the resistance. Consequently, order was sent by a glider-borne personal courier from London to destroy the station.

Section Apeldoorn, under whose command I still was operating, knew that I had participated in drawing up blueprints for a transmitting station which the German engineers were building to be installed in the north German town of Bremen.

With my knowledge of electronics in short-wave radio

and telex communications, I was able to sabotage the drawings in almost unnoticeable ways. Accordingly, I was selected, with two other men, to execute a plan that would blow the station sky-high.

For three weeks, we were instructed and drilled by men who really knew their trade. We were then issued a car with false license plates, forged identification papers and an utter determination to be successful. This determination was reinforced by the considerable amount of dynamite sticks that had been stashed under the back seat of our car. With this baggage, we set out in the direction of the Southwest.

The weather was perfect for the situation — miserably cold and damp, and snow accompanied us all day long. This type of weather should have been an ideal opportunity for the Germans for winter training, in case they were sent off to the snowy steppes of Russia. However, most of them preferred to stay in the warmth of their barracks.

At the border crossing between the provinces of Brabant and Zeeland, we were stopped by a German military police patrol which demanded to see our identification papers. Apparently, the papers were perfect imitations because, after some sardonic smiles and whispers, the Germans let us continue on our risky mission.

When we crossed the canal that separated the island from the mainland, we extinguished our black-out headlights and waited behind one of the many dikes until total darkness engulfed us. A moonless night and a cloud-covered sky were to be our guardians.

Some time later, in total darkness, we proceeded on our journey, arriving precisely at 6:30 p.m. at our destination. One-hundred-and-fifty yards now separated us from the sitting-duck target behind a fence. The real engagement had begun! Hans, one of our partners, was to stay in the car, while Peter, the other partner, and I were to operate on the actual terrain.

To be as silent as possible, we took off our shoes, so

On a harrowing mission in Holland

that the snow would not crunch under our feet.

Due to the inclement weather and the evening meal time, only one man stood guard at the main entrance. For us, a German in sight was better than two in the latrine! However, we did not waste time worrying about the consequences of being caught.

We crawled to the fence, cut the wire mesh and, like two snakes in the grass, wiggled inside the station compound. The sticks of dynamite that made Sweden's Mr. Nobel so rich that we now confer prizes in his honor each year, dangled around our necks like giant sausages, ready to prove Mr. Nobel's chemical formula.

The noise coming from the generators of the station made it quite easy for us to find the main building. At the back of the structure, we found the iron door that led to the furnace room. The door was unlocked. Peter signaled me to descend with him into the dark abyss, which I did, closing the door behind me.

In total darkness, we groped our way down the staircase into the unknown. Further down, I finally dared to light a match that showed us the way. A snug warmth greeted us on the downward trek, but there was no time to feel comfortable. With controlled nervousness, we selected a place above the generators where we would bundle and lay our sticks of "silence."

We had done it so often in training that fastening the dynamite load to the ceiling of the furnace room was purely a matter of routine. The procedure went so smoothly that we were some minutes ahead of our schedule and were able to take our time to connect the 150-yard-long ignition cable.

It seemed an eternity before we returned to the cellar steps. Arriving at the top of the stairs, I opened the iron door slowly and was greatly relieved not to be looking down the barrel of a rifle. On the contrary, it was as quiet on the Zeeland front as Christmas Eve in the Alps.

We took exactly the same way back, following our

easily visible footprints. We were filled with a feeling of confidence and satisfaction of a job well done. As I unrolled the cable from the reel, Peter covered it up with snow and we, again, exited through the hole we had cut in the mesh fencing.

We couldn't resist looking back and I will always remember the lonesome German guard, stomping his feet trying to warm himself. Little did he know that very soon, he would indeed be very warm without stomping!

Returning to the car back on the country road, where Hans was nervously biting his nails, I proceeded to connect the end of the cable to the ignition mechanism. We did not talk all the while, remembering the proverb that "Speech is silver, silence is golden."

The car stood headed in the direction of the small town of Kapelle, which would be our destination after the explosion and where we would go into hiding at the home of a local farmer who had been informed about our action and was expecting us. Hans took his place behind the wheel and I took my place on the seat beside him. The moment had now come for which we had been selected to do our patriotic duty.

Only now did we feel the strange nervousness that was a combination of fear and uncertainty. Darkness settled upon us and we could not see one another's face. It seemed ages before we acknowledged that we were indeed looking at each other, hoping for mutual consent to give the final touch.

Suddenly, the "third man," Peter, pushed down the handle of the ignition, as if he were pumping air into a bicycle tire. The immediate explosion in the main building was so vehement that the air pressure from the blast shook the car. For a moment, we gazed in fascination at what we had brought about. Then, Peter jumped into the back seat of the car and before the door had slammed shut, we were speeding along the narrow country road toward Kapelle. Peter, in his great hurry, had forgotten his "bicycle pump" but in the world of 1944, our lives were more important than an ignition gadget left at the roadside.

After several minutes, I turned around to look back through the rear window. Apart from an immense pillar of fire, there was no sign of the enemy in hot pursuit. Did we hit a home run?

Ten minutes later, we arrived at the farm where the farmer had constructed a large haystack in such a manner that we were able to drive right into it, stopping directly under the cap.

The farmer had quickly concealed our presence by covering the entrance with great masses of hay. Just in time, we noticed, because the German military police, on their motorcycles with sidecars, were close upon our heels.

Innocently, the farmer and his wife stood by the side of the road and waved as the searchers whizzed by at high speed. We had a fearful and sleepless night as the constant roar of the cycles droned past the farmhouse over and over again.

Even to catnap was impossible because the stifling heat and the smell of hay gave little chance for comfort. The next day, the farmer released us from our self-imposed prison and took us into the farmhouse where we remained for three days, hiding in the attic which had double floorboards.

In our "captivity," we spent the time of day talking and eating. To our great relief, we were not discovered, despite two visits to the farm by the military police.

On the evening of the third day, the farmer scouted the area by bicycle to see if the coast was clear. Upon his return, he told us that there was no immediate danger, as far as he could judge.

We "undressed" the car, filled our tank with the farmer's black market gasoline and continued our mission to the next island, called Walcheren. It was 12:30 p.m. — the noon hour — so, nestled between the other cars on the road, we were as inconspicuous as a black man in a South

African homeland.

Again, we found billeting in the home of a farmer who gave us food and clothed us in typical farmer's blue overalls, complete with cap and wooden shoes. The picture was perfect and it proved once again that clothes make the man! We worked the fields for three days, side-by-side with the farmer and in spite of the many passing German patrols, our disguise did not spark curiosity.

On the sixth day after the explosion, we bade the farmer's family good-bye and took a different route back to Apeldoorn. Tired, several pounds lighter and some years older in experience, we learned that our mission had been successful and that the station was totally disabled.

This would be the end of the story, were it not for a very bizarre sequel. Some 20 years later, I was engaged at the Opera House in West Berlin, where I struck up a friendship with Peter Roth-Ehrang, one of the leading basses there. After several months, he "confessed" to me that, to his great regret, he had belonged to the German occupational forces in Holland. He assured me, however, that he had never used a gun because he was working at a radio station in the province of Zeeland.

My heart started to pound. Could it be possible? Yes, it could! Peter Roth-Ehrang had narrowly escaped the devastating explosion. When I told him "who done it," we both wept profusely.

Then he proceeded to tell his story and I told him mine. We could not now, as friends, conceive the idea that at one time we wanted to blow out each other's "life candle." For weeks, we discussed every detail and marvelled over the coincidence of our meeting.

Why do people heap so much grief upon each other when there is so much to live for?

Peter died three months later of cancer.

I had lost a good comrade.

Chapter Nine

Music, molasses and pancakes bring brief truce

In the midst of World War II, during the winter of 1943, to be precise, a neighbor in The Hague told me he had a nephew who ran a flower bulb business in the small town of Rynsburg (Rhine Castle) just north of the historic city of Leyden on the Rhine River.

It may come as a surprise to some readers, but the Rhine River is not a German monopoly. It has its source in Switzerland, and gets most of its chemical pollution from French and German factories before finally "enriching" The Netherlands with the contaminated liquid leftovers of what once was clear, natural glacier water.

My mother, always scintillating at difficult moments, suggested that a life of nourishing tulip bulbs was certainly of great value to a "war-boy" of those privational years. So, one cold morning in December, I bicycled 50 miles north to the neat, very much Dutch Reformed village of said Rynsburg, where 300 years earlier the great Dutch rabbi and philosopher Spinoza had spent two years writing his life work, *The Principles of Descartes and the Metaphysic*. Finding the bulb farm and my neighbor's nephew was quickly done. I told him about my mother's culinary desires for a few bags of retired flower bulbs.

The farmer was of the humanitarian sort, so having deposited the bulbs in a paper container and having chatted at length about the defiled time that we were "privileged" to live in, he finally invited me to stay for lunch. I accepted with avidity because a Rynsburger bulb farmer in those years could offer more life-saving ingredients than a Rockefeller or Getty could offer in their glory days.

The rumor going around in the big cities, that the farmers in the country were still able to put butter and bacon on the table, proved to be true.

Hardly had the farmer's wife, Alie, served some old-fashioned oatmeal on my plate, when we heard a knock on the front door. When the farmer opened the door, there stood a German soldier on the threshold, wearing the notoriously familiar uniform, a terrifying rifle over his shoulder and sporting nickel "national health" glasses on his pale nose. In an inconsequential tone, he told the perplexed farmer that his name was Heinrich and that he was instructed to be the "watchdog" of three Russian POWs who were "repairing" an intact road as a make-work task for a punishment squad.

"Hello," said the farmer, "my name is Henk and that's Dutch for Heinrich." Glad that they at least had one thing in common, Heinrich exposed a set of gold fillings during his return smile and asked the Dutch Henk if he had something with which to fill his hungry stomach.

Observing the blind stare on Henk's face, I helpfully translated what the German had said into Dutch. Henk looked in matrimonial dependence at his wife, Alie, because it was she who wore the pants at home, as I later perceived. However, in this unfamiliar situation, Alie thought it was more advisable to "return" the pants to her husband, which she promptly did by staring stalwartly at her still-empty plate.

An uneasy silence wafted through the small room, as if warning of troubles to come. I looked at the deceitfully peaceful-looking Krupp rifle and thought that it was time to take action. To keep the diplomatic channels open, I suggested to Henk and Alie that a bite of food could, perhaps, prevent us from hard labor in Germany and also, from joining the three Russians in their toil on the road, because obviously Heinrich was the one with the gun.

Henk walked slowly up to Heinrich, puffing out his wiry 6-foot frame and looking Heinrich square in the eye, as if

Music, molasses and pancakes bring brief truce

he had Mohammed Ali in front of him. He said strongly, in perfectly articulated "double Dutch," "I will give you food on one condition; that the three Russians join us in the table feast." I translated the offer to the armed enemy, but speculated that being the underdog, it was rather naive and perilous to try to make a deal.

Henk, with patriotic perseverance, expecting at any moment a Germanic outburst, faced the coming danger with equanimity. Far from the mark! Heinrich's hunger was much more gnawing than his imperious hostility and Hank's request was royally granted.

Smiling from ear to ear, Heinrich walked back to the door, stuck two fingers in his mouth and whistled to the Russians to come closer as if he were calling his dogs to heel. With astonished but suspicious expressions on their fatigued faces, Lenin's disciples entered the farmer's house. Helmet and woolen caps were removed in response to a single glance that could not be disobeyed, from the piercing eyes of the fidgeting Alie.

With the unmistakably universal word "sit" and additional vague gesticulations, the farmer summoned everybody to sit down at the table. Alie, however, in taking the pants back from her husband again, walked up to the washbasin with the four foreigners in her wake and did not leave room for misinterpretation, as she pressed a bar of soap in the German's hand. After having washed his hands, he passed the soap on to his Russian foes.

Back at the table, it was inevitable that in the shadow of Leyden, the cradle of conservative Dutch Calvinism, the farmer would ask everyone to fold their hands and close their eyes in saying Grace, for good companionship.

For Stalin's grenadiers, this was a hard nut to crack. But in exchange for pancakes with butter, beacon and molasses, axioms were thrown overboard at once, just as if atheism had not been the fundamental principle of Marx's teachings. Similarly, but five years previous to the founding of the U.N., the Dutch Reformed farmer and his tractable wife, plus the three Russians, raised in godlessness, the Nazi warrior and little me, were surrounding the dining room table as if peace on earth had become a fact of life. In spite of the lack of *sauerkraut* and *stroganoff*, the four enemies ate to their hearts' content, filling themselves with never-ending pancakes. There was not much talk during the meal, but in the midst of a mouthful of pancake, one of the Russians detected a small treadle-organ standing almost abandoned in the adjacent and rather oppressive Sunday parlor. For a devoted Dutch Reformed farmer in those years, it was a *must* to have a small treadle-organ in one's home, even if the owner could only play *Chopsticks*.

Russia's discarded warrior slowly got up from his chair and walked into the cold organ room, while chewing his pancake. Without pressing down the keys, his weather-beaten fingers caressed the yellow ivory of the keyboard as if it were a newborn baby.

The German now judged the time ripe to start an argument as to who, in point of fact, was here the representative of the invincible 1,000-year empire. "Sit down at once," he ordered in a harsh tone. But the Russian was also not born yesterday, and thoroughly conscious of being on neutral ground, he tossed in return a frightfully sounding response that only his compatriots understood.

For a moment, dark clouds loomed on the horizon, but the astute farmer broke the deadlock by walking up to the Russian and shaking his hand as if he had just made a home run.

The Cossack looked sternly into Hank's eyes, trying to detect a meaning behind the handshake, but then a vague smile wafted over his characteristic face and he pointed to the ring on his finger. Then, speaking in a totally incomprehensibly guttural sound, he managed to make it clear that he did not want to exchange his ring for more pancakes, but that he was referring to his wife in far-off Russia.

By pointing in turn first to his ring and then to the silent organ, he made us understand at once that his wife also played an instrument, although an organ in atheistic Bolshevik Russia seemed just as out of place in those days as a synagogue in Germany.

The Russian ice was broken and every one of us tried to put his two cents worth into the international pot of understanding.

Heinrich then asked me if I lived in Rynsburg. I answered in the negative but proudly told him that my cradle had stood in one of the most beautiful cities of the world, The Hague, and added, ambiguously, "It can't be much if it ain't Dutch."

To bring our pancake festivities to a climax, I walked into the organ room, sat down on the organ stool and, after having pumped the bellows with my feet, I started to play some improvisations on the willing instrument. Little by little, the entire pancake party arranged itself around the organ, its sounds bringing with it an association of the approaching Christmas time.

I remembered, just in time, that I could sing and play Stephen Adams' *The Holy City* from memory and so, without further ado, I sang the song in the forbidden English language.

"Jerusalem, Jerusalem," I sang and they all understood. That Jerusalem was in Palestine and that Jesus was a Jew did not even bother the indoctrinated German. When I finished my last "Hosanna for evermore," I looked around me and saw that the Russians, as well as the German warrior, were on the point of breaking down on their knees. Entire waterworks of sadness and loneliness rolled down their international cheeks. So, quickly smelling the agony of success, I threw in the greatest emotional hit of all times, *Silent Night*.

A performing artist has to strike when the iron is hot! "*Danke, danke,*" said the German, "*Schön war das.*" And the sobbing Russians also said things that they mutually agreed upon. I "encored" some more well-placed songs and friend and foe sang a few times with me as if we were sitting around a campfire on Noah's Ark.

Sometime later, in a tone of impermeable amity, Heinrich informed his three Russians that "lunchtime" was over and so was fraternization. The road workers were rounded up again, under the motto: "He that buildeth in the street, many masters has to meet."

Half an hour later, I pedaled my bike with wooden tires past the place where the POWs' punitive expedition was repairing a road that had never been damaged in the first place. Like lifelong friends, we grinned at one another and the bricklaying activities were interrupted until I, waving frantically, vanished from sight.

War god Mars must have been on vacation that day in Rynsburg when Hitler's and Stalin's fusiliers were peaceful and unconcerned.

Music is the road to international understanding, but so are pancakes with molasses.

Chapter Ten

Holland is finally liberated, but not before some parting atrocities

From late 1944 onward, the German armies introduced a new weapon into the wintry sky over Western Europe. The guided missile turned every day into a Fourth of July fireworks display with deadly consequences.

A certain Herr Wernherr von Braun, a German scientist of Russian military nobleman extraction, had the ingenuity to develop and put into use a rocket that was the forerunner of Redstones, Titans and other deadly toys.

His brainchild was clearly intended to turn the tide in the lost Ocean of Nazism. Although his V-2 long-range liquid fuel rockets were constructed in Peenemunde, a North German seacoast town, and were aimed at the British Isles, most of its victims were in Holland.

The imperfect monsters were launched by Herr von Braun and his colleagues from four ramps in Western Holland. Unfortunately, one of the launch sites was only two miles behind the house of my parents. A peaceful soccer field had undergone a metamorphosis and was transformed into an launch site for murderous war mechanisms.

For several hours every day, the 70-foot-long monstrosities were slung into the air, embarking on their mission of doom and destruction. However, the imperfection of the rockets didn't take them very far. One-half of them went up only to come down again after a few miles of flight, creating panic wherever the slow and low-flying monsters passed over, sowing death and perdition.

When the rockets struck the ground, many thousands had to die as a result of von Braun's lunacy that was created to change the war in favor of Hitler's warmongers.

Unlike the thousands of innocent victims, von Braun survived the war. However, unlike his compatriots who had also committed, in their ways, horrific crimes and atrocities against mankind, he was not put on the dock at the Nuremberg Trials in 1945. For European survivors, it has been a hard-to-swallow reality that along with Barbie, Waldheim and other alleged Nazi war criminals, von Braun was not tried. Instead, like Barbie in 1945, he was whisked away to the U.S.A. to work as a technical adviser and developer for the U.S. rocket programs in Alabama and New Mexico.

He was welcomed and even honored by presidents and other honorable and honest dignitaries. He died in 1977, a naturalized U.S. citizen, unashamed that his actions during the war were disastrous and deadly to half the seeds of Europe.

When the survivors of the war years in Nazi-occupied Europe took note of von Braun's elevation to U.S. citizenship, they simply could not understand it. But what did they know about politics?

Meanwhile, the victorious American army had penetrated the Siegfried Line and was coming closer day-by-day, as we learned through daily news bulletins from the forbidden station, Radio London. Rumors had it that our liberation was imminent and would presumably take place during the third week of October 1944. The entire nation became euphoric.

Free, free, free again! Butter, footballs and bicycle tires. Peace is the essence of a good life.

Like in World War I, the Belgian Ardennes were to become the site of the decisive battle of victory or defeat. The last important German offensive of World War II began in December 1944. Field Marshal von Rundstedt launched a surprise attack and the Battle of the Bulge was born.

The U.S. Third Army started a counterattack from the south and the First Army did the same from the north. Three

Holland is finally liberated...

weeks later, 120,000 of von Rundstedt's soldiers were sacrificed to the *Volk, Vaterland und Führer*. The Yankees had never been more popular in the low countries of Flanders and Holland.

Fully expecting that Holland's liberation by U.S. troops was just around the corner, the German occupying forces started to plunder the big cities before retreating into their homeland.

That tens of thousands of bicycles, radios and other valuables were stolen could not dampen the exhilaration brought on by the prospect of impending freedom. The Allied High Command, however, had other intentions. Alas! Concerned by the fast advance of their allied friends, the Russians on the Eastern front, the Western commanders decided not to go north and liberate Belgium and Holland but, instead, to turn east into Germany via Remagen.

With the Allied forces blowing Nazi Germany off the face of the earth, the remaining skeleton of the once-victorious German Army was aware that at this time, Holland would be a safer place than their own country. With every single soldier carrying stolen goods on stolen bicycles, they already were on the move when word came of the change of plans by the U.S. First Army. The retreating Germans thus made a 180 degree turn and went back to the Dutch barracks that they had so nefariously abandoned.

This chaotic return some days after the "liberation" that had been so frenetically celebrated was a terrible blow for every peace-loving Dutchman. The German forces returned on a Tuesday and, to this very day, the so-called *Dolle Dinsdag* (Frantic Tuesday) is commemorated in Holland.

For the next five months, the Nazi occupational regime reigned again with a deadly iron fist and punished the people who could do nothing about the situation. When finally the Canadian troops liberated The Netherlands from the Nazi yoke, many people still had to die by the Nazi sword before the "closing hour."

Despite the unconditional surrender of all German

forces at Reims, France, 22 German war fanatics decided to die an "heroic" death on that fateful day in May 1945. They entrenched themselves in several towers around Dam Square in the center of Amsterdam. At 8 p.m., at the height of the liberation festivities, with every Amsterdam citizen dancing and singing, the Germans opened fire with rifles and machine-guns. For 20 long minutes, before taking their own lives, the murderers scattered a spray of deadly bullets that resulted in the massacre of nearly 270 people within sight of the harbor lights.

One week before, in an orgy of destruction, German troops had blown up the protective dikes in the province of Zeeland. This corn belt of Holland exists entirely of islands and has the most fertile soil in the country. Some 250,000 people had to flee to the mainland from the destructive, roaring masses of salt water. But 1,800 did not make it in time. Eighty-four percent of Zeeland was inundated or made inaccessible by landmines left behind by the occupiers.

Forty-five hundred homes were destroyed when the pounding surf of sea water flooded and poisoned the once so fruitful soil which had served mankind for 700 years.

For many years after World War II, the aftereffects of this dastardly feat were still the order of the day in the farming province of Zeeland. In 1950, however, the Dutch government decided to close all estuaries with gigantic, cement caissons.

The colossal Delta Works to save southern Holland from future flooding took 36 years to complete. In 1986, Queen Beatrix of The Netherlands declared the Delta Works completed. Having attended the ceremonies, it made me feel good that farmlands of Zeeland have been restored and the scars of war have finally faded. The bestial memories, however, will never be forgotten by those who have known this devastation.

Chapter Eleven

Fighting off starvation as war ends

As an exhausting World War II lingered on in Europe, and Germany was now annihilated from the air and on the ground, only three-quarters of Holland had been liberated by Canadian forces.

The three most populated western provinces, including Amsterdam, Rotterdam and The Hague, were still occupied by German armies that had nothing to fight for anymore, but still would not surrender. The allied forces, though, had more important battles to fight inside the German Reich, than to go through the time-consuming task of unchaining some two million hungry people from despotism.

Thus, January, February and March of 1945 were three of the most difficult months of my entire life. The whole nation was on its last legs. There was no electricity anymore, nor gasoline; no train transportation, nor taxis. Food was a word that was reminiscent of bygone days. Through the ingenuity and cunning of some, however, people managed to dodge the threat of death from starvation.

Cattle and pigs, horses, fowl and other fountains of lifesaving nourishment had long since been consumed or stolen by the enemy and transported to Germany which was now, also, in ultimate disarray.

Dogs and cats once more proved to be "man's best friend" as they had to give their lives to serve as dinner for humanity.

One article, originally created to spread beauty, the flower bulb, was now destined to serve as a culinary lifesaver. People who, in peacetime, had stood in line waiting to view and sniff at the orgy of colors comprising Holland's most admired product of the springtime, were now lining up to buy bulbs to use as nourishment.

Tulip bulbs, hyacinth bulbs, daffodils and narcissus have not only different forms, color and smell when they bloom, but they also differ in taste, as we soon found out. The cooking range, in homes of those days, was a 12-inch-high, square stove with air holes in the sides, ironically called "the giant." On the stove bottom, kindling wood was placed and burned, producing the necessary heat for cooking.

Every day, hundreds of worried wives and mothers could be seen scouring the woods for dry sticks to be used in their mini-stoves. Sugar beets and turnips, used for cattle fodder in peacetime, were now, for lack of our four-legged dairy producers, being elevated to a *bonne bouche*, which was a dainty delicacy that adorned the dinner plates at night.

Three times a week, a single-page newspaper could be purchased. One ignored the front page which still hollered the achievements of the great war. However, on the reverse side was printed a much awaited column, called *The Art of Cookery*, with numerous "bulb" recipes.

The following was a typical recipe for four persons:

PANCAKE NATURELLE

- Take 40 hyacinth bulbs and one sugar beet.
- Remove outer skin from bulbs and grind the bulbs in a meat grinder until tender.
- Separate pulp from juice, saving the liquid. The addition of salt is not recommended because it might raise blood pressure. (Nobody had salt, anyway.)
- Start the fire in your "giant" range.
- Grease a pre-warmed saucepan with the sugar beet juice and, when warm enough, spread the "bulb-porridge" over the bottom of the pan and bake.
- To enhance the taste, it is recommended to sprinkle half of the grated sugar beet over the porridge.

Have a pleasant meal!

Fighting off starvation as war ends

Today, a cow with any dignity would shrug her udders at such a meal, but in times of extreme necessity, "one bulb on the plate is better than 1,000 bulbs in the field."

Men, still addicted to their habit of smoking, made "tobacco" from the leftover outer bulb skins, by rubbing the leaves between the palms of their hands until pulverized enough to roll it in a piece of newspaper. The rolled cigarette was glued together with the naturally sticky sugar beet juice.

The home-made coffin-nails were named SABTO which would-be poets translated into "Stinks Awful, Better Try Others!" There were also "real" cigarettes in circulation on the black market for $75 a package!

Most families were afflicted with ailments from malnutrition and many suffered losses as a result of this. In our family, my father was seized with a ghastly blood poisoning. This first manifested itself through carbuncles all over his body. Eventually, he developed bone cancer which was attributed to malnutrition. A once dynamic and vigorous man was doomed to a passive existence and merely wasted away.

In a nation whose fertile fields had once been one of most abundant food producers of the world, starving people could be found lying in doorways and dying in other public places, on streets and squares. The population languished, unequaled in its suffering.

In three month's time, more lives were lost than during the entire Eighty-year-war (1568-1648) with Spain. Finally, under extreme pressure from the International Red Cross in Geneva, its Swedish president, Count Bernadotte, chartered 50 commercial airplanes and had them filled to the hilt with loaves of bread.

As later, in the heroic U.S. airlift in 1948 to save Berlin from the Russian blockade, hundreds of "bread-plane" flights took place, flying Missions of Manna for a steady two weeks over the distressed cities of western Holland, delivering food to a starving people.

Since food supplies for the German forces were cut off as well, they also shared in the agony of hunger. Standing side-by-side with the uniformed enemy on the rooftops of Dutch apartment houses, gathering "manna from heaven" together, was a completely new manifestation of solidarity in the final hours of the war.

For the first time in five years, Germans tried to speak Dutch and the Hollanders took notice of their efforts as we were now all in the same boat, fighting for survival. The common enemy now was hunger and not anymore human hostility, inasmuch as the inclination of forbearance passes through the stomach.

Hunger causes intolerance, turmoil and disobedience, which leads to uprising and civic unrest and the wish to overthrow the ruling power, irrespective of political direction.

Hunger has no political claims but is bedded in hollow eyes, unbearable suffering and destruction. I survived, with millions of my compatriots, those brutal five years of inhumane debasement. Yet, an unconquerable fear that history may repeat itself, that "your youngest and strongest will fall by the sword," will not give me rest.

Chapter Twelve

What to do when the war has ended?

The Thousand Year Empire that was predicted by Herr Schicklgruber (alias Adolf Hitler) in his futuristic thriller *Mein Kampf* (*My Battle*), written in 1927, while imprisoned in Landsberg in Bavaria, had after 18 dreadful years gone down the drain like in fatuous nightmare.

It was the spring of 1945 and in the lowlands of Europe, a wondrous miracle had come to pass: Peace! No one could envision what the future had in store. What a challenge! Having survived these five long, exhausting years of war, we now would surely be able to adjust to the years of peace, as well.

Free again! No need to kill any more. What should I undertake? Where should I go? Is there anyone who needs me? Is there a brochure on how to get along in post-wartime? Complete freedom! Fascism, communism? Who needs Left — who needs Right?

Life has started to pulsate once more after having been strangled for five whole years. When one gets past a certain age in life, a period of five years slips by like the shadow of an airplane, fast but noiselessly.

Five years of day-to-day tyranny, however, drags interminably and would torment any young lad, as it tormented me in the throes of puberty.

It was finally "after the war" and we were stuck with the leftovers. Many of us had the feeling of taking a sunbath after a swim in the ocean. Wonderfully refreshing, but when one lies down on the beach, there is a lot of scratchy sand sticking to the body.

The hackneyed attitude of "I'll do that when the war is

over" was now past tense and zero hour of peace had arrived! Would someone now stop me at the next street corner and say, "Young fella; you didn't do too badly during the lousy war years. You rightly refused to obey the laws forced on you by the enemy, so let me show you the rules to follow now that peace has broken out!"

Big deal! There were no rules, nor precepts. "My country, right or wrong" had proven to be the ultimate miscalculation for the German people.

Holland now had to establish the appropriate objectives of a democratic society in an postwar vacuum. All the vows that we had promised ourselves to keep when the day of Freedom should arrive were waiting to be fulfilled.

Over the past five years, every well-disposed Dutchman knew the psychologically humiliating effect of being picked up off the streets by the Gestapo.

Many a "patriot" who took the easy road of neutrality during the occupation, now suddenly became a flag-waver and absorbed himself in the search for collaborators who had violated the rules of common ethics.

Now that they were unopposed, these peacetime "heroes," fed their egos by apprehending the girls who had been in intimate collaboration with the occupying enemy. These maidens were nicknamed "German mattresses," as many of them had spent most of the war years in a horizontal position, in exchange for butter, chocolate, stockings or just entertainment.

The result came nine months later. The uniformed fathers were sent to the Russian front but the mothers were left behind with their "butter babies."

Those women were later forced from their homes by the would-be Dutch patriots and, having been forced to ride on horse-drawn carts through the streets of their community, they were put on public display. Arriving at the village square, they were seated in chairs while their heads were totally shaven.

What to do when the war has ended?

After this humiliating act, the women were tied to a pillory for 24 hours, thus giving the newly-liberated townsfolk an opportunity for cheap retaliation. They were duly spat upon and pelted with rotten tomatoes and clods of mud, using the girls' faces as proverbial dart boards.

Our beloved ancestors from the "Golden Middle Ages" would have jumped for joy at the same opportunity. "Let anyone among you who is without sin be the first to throw a stone at her." *John 8:7.*

Those countrymen who, in 1940, had the financial means to escape the occupation by taking refuge in England, at this time returned to their homeland, convinced that their absence had been duly noticed

Now, the fatherland was unstained again and expectations were high. The sky was cloudless-blue and one could once more freely breathe in the sweet smell of jasmine.

Hundreds of times we had promised ourselves that we would make up for the lost years and do everything totally different and better. Building a glorious future was only a drop in the rain shower of ambition. No substitutions anymore! Everything would be real!

The coffee, the bicycle tires and people. What luxuries. What abundance. What a life lay ahead of us all, myself included. Shall I leave home and seek adventure in Polynesia, New Zealand or Tahiti? I would discover the world, speak foreign languages, become acquainted with strange cultures, have women, drinking bouts, smoke mind-stretching but artery-closing nicotine!

Kick over the traces of the past and be wanton. Sensation, adventure, the dreaming of faraway places and lasciviousness. An immeasurable, wild future. What a divine life! Stop the world, I've started to live!

As it turned out, I was to return to the monotonous, dead-silent boredom of the drawing board at the Dutch Telephone and Telegraph Service and remain there for another five years.

Chapter Thirteen

A tenor joins the Royal Conservatory

On a November evening in 1947, I was invited to the home of friends whom the money-god, Mammon, had not overlooked when dealing out the purses.

Having reached the enviable years where the Patron Saint of covetousness was closer to me than algebra or geometry, it had not escaped my drowsy glances that the daughter of the house was an extremely enchanting example of the fair sex. She was not only lovely to behold but had a singing voice to match. Her father was the spitting image of the famous conductor Leopold Stokowsky, and was also born in the same city, Krakow, Poland.

The family saw this coincidence as a good reason for organizing a monthly evening of art and entertainment in its mansion of 27 rooms. On that particular evening they had invited, among others, Eduard van Beinum, the principal conductor of the Amsterdam Concertgebouw Orchestra, and also a fascinating personality in the form of Josephine Baker who happened to be in town.

Although she was born in St. Louis, Josephine lived and made her career mainly in Paris where she was the idol of countless bachelors and, also, former bachelors. Her *piece-de-resistance* was a show in which she wore only 69 bananas.

Josephine's shows in the famous Lido of Paris were a constant sellout and were particularly visited by Frenchmen who turned "bananas" at the sight of those yellow fruits decorating that curvaceous brown female body. I asked her in my youthful innocence, if she had brought her "peep-show-fruit" along, in anticipation of her singing answer, "No, we have no bananas, we have no bananas today."

My question, unfortunately, went down like a ton of bricks, judging by the devastating glance shot my way. Only on-stage did Josephine show the fruit from the farmers' market, so on that night in November, she played the upright daughter of Prudence and the mother of 12 adopted children.

Probably as a homage to her Spanish-born father, she treated us to some Spanish ballads that no one understood. As a follow-up, my lovely girlfriend, whom I had often entertained with a serenade during sailing tours, persuaded me to demonstrate my ability in the field of vocal recreation.

When I was 15 years old, my mother had taught me a German song by Franz Schubert, which always came in handy for occasions such as this, because nobody knew that it was the only classical song that I could perform in a foreign language.

After having brought Schubert's product to a relatively successful ending, an earnest but gloomy-looking man got up from his chair and walked over to me. He had the compelling personality of someone who is accustomed to having his thoughts read and put directly into action, preferably yesterday.

"Well sung, young fella," he said in a fatherly manner — that is as far as his disposition allowed him to go.

"You've got something with that voice of yours, you really have something there!" He was, as I soon discovered, Dr. Albert Plesman, founder and director-general of KLM, the Royal Dutch Airlines, now one of the leading companies of the world.

Before I was able to modestly contradict his judgment, he had walked away from me, returning a moment later with Eduard van Beinum hanging on his arm, as if he were about to introduce his fiancée.

"Eddie," he said with a confidential air, "this fella should take up singing and you have to give him a leg up." van Beinum was a very handsome man with a mane of Clairol-black, curly hair and a smile that could melt the Arctic Ocean.

Although he had worked for many years with "real" singers, he gave me the diplomatic compliment that Schubert songs are hard to beat. Not to be deterred, Plesman led him by the nose and pressed van Beinum to promise me that I would hear from him soon. He kept his word and later in my career, I sang often under his baton.

Some months later, I received in imposing-looking letter from the Royal Conservatory of The Hague, my hometown, with the stimulating news that I was expected to appear at that place at a given time and date and to bring my own music scores with me.

When I arrived at the "musical instruction institute," I was led immediately to the office of the director. My knees quivered under me, much like I imagine an amateur football player trembles when he is asked to pay his first respects to the Miami Dolphin's boss, Don Shula.

Nervous as a racehorse, I hoped the jury was not going to ask me what *allegro sostonuto* or G sharp minor was, because that was Chinese to me.

As I entered the director's office, an elderly, artistic looking, white-haired gentleman approached me with thoughtful steps. His circular-shaped face and rosy cheeks gave him the appearance of kindheartedness that one would only attribute to Santa Claus.

He smiled at me like a physician who always knows better and grabbed me by the arm. I was steered into a room where, behind a long table, sat five extremely white-haired gentlemen, all expensive-looking without an exception, making up the committee that was to judge my abilities.

I felt much like Humphrey Bogart's character, Captain Queeg in *The Caine Mutiny*, standing in front of a court martial jury, except that I lacked the calming effect of rolling marbles in my fist. The friendly man who still held my arm as if he wanted to keep it, told me in a hoarse voice that his name was Sam Dresden, and that he was the director of the Royal Conservatory.

I decided that the time was ripe for a return smile, but when he introduced the white-haired members of the music session council, I turned chalk-white. They all were, in my humble opinion, terribly famous names with equally sagacious people behind them. I had not known their faces but every single name was a billboard name to me.

A disappearing act, or simply to evaporate, was out of question, so I was forced to face the music. "What is a name?" said a contemptible voice low in my stomach. "They have to boil water the same way as I do." When finally the first question came up, it was a load off my mind.

"What are you going to sing for us?" asked Santa Claus Dresden. Feeling like a condemned man in front of a firing squad, I decided to go down with dignity and give the best that I had to offer — my voice!

Without any hesitation, I sang the beautiful aria to the *Evening Star* from Richard Wagner's opera, *Tannhauser*. Little did I know that, first, this aria should be sung by a baritone, which I was not, and, second, by a much stronger voice than I had at that time.

How should I have known that my voice type was not at all suited for this opera?! I had hardly sung half-a-minute when a snickering Prof. Dr. Lothar Wallerstein interrupted my clumsy foray into the world of Wagner. Wallerstein knew his "oats," since he not only was a surgeon but also a brilliant pianist, stage director and conductor who even substituted for Toscanini once at the Metropolitan Opera. In short, he knew what he was laughing about when he heard my awkward conversion as a "baritone."

"Please," he tittered, and in a very Germanically-interwoven Dutch said, "Sing a scale for us, yes?" I asked the pianist to give me any given tone on the piano. Going higher after each completed scale, I was rudely interrupted by another panel member with the warning, "If you go one scale higher, you will not be able to come down anymore."

The entire panel seemed highly entertained but I felt more like Danny Kaye in *The Court Jester*. However, the panel's humor was not unfounded because my vocal scales had arrived in the tenoral stratosphere and had long surpassed the notorious High C!

"You are not a baritone," chortled Prof. Wallerstein, "but a very high tenor!" "High winds blow on high hills," added another panel member, chuckling as if to give me the weather report. This man with the Italian name Ravelli, was not only the personification of a typical matter-of-fact Dutchman but he was also, at that time, one of the most sought-after concert singers in Europe. He wore rimless FDR glasses and had the old-fashioned looks of an Albert Einstein. He later became my first voice teacher.

I had to go through the entire wear and tear of the full examination with possible and impossible questions. If I did not know the answer to a question, the five men behind the table remained in high spirits and were even receptive to some of my more embarrassingly fanciful replies. After three hours, I felt as though I had been brainwashed.

Then, the white-haired troupe moved into a circle like the time-out formation of a basketball team and started whispering as if telling obscene jokes. Assuming that I had failed the test, I bravely collected some lost dignity and prepared myself for the worst. To my great delight, however, Sam Dresden, the director, announced that although I did not qualify to be considered as the new Caruso, the Department of Culture of The Netherlands was gracious enough to award me a scholarship enabling me to study at the Royal Conservatory for the next four years at the Dutch taxpayers' expense. My musical future had begun.

With apologies to my countrymen, I can set them at ease. Their money was well spent.

Chapter Fourteen

Learning to sing from the great masters

Nineteen-fifty marked a turning point for me. I exchanged the drawing board at the P.T.T. for the stage of my musical future I had finally freed myself from the confining straight jacket of bureaucratic pressure and had decided henceforth to swim on the strength of my own boldness. At that moment, however, I was more or less floating on my own scrawny frame, rather than living off the fat of the land.

I was, though, ambitious and emulous enough to spread my raw-boned wings like a young inexperienced eagle. Little by little, the embryo of what is popularly called a "career" loomed on the horizon and I honed my artistic swimming skills weekly in the pool of musical commotion. Even swimming upstream soon became one of my preferable qualities and I cherish these attributes to this day.

My music conservatory years in The Hague were not among the most passive days of my life. It became more and more apparent that a federal grant of 300 Dutch guilders per annum was not going to change my old bicycle into a Cadillac on my daily trips to and from the music institution. My financial status was so meager that I was forced to continue my position an as electrotechnical draftsman with the Postal Telephone and Telegraph Co. of The Netherlands. This governmental enterprise with its 30,000 employees but without any computers, was blessed with a tenacious team of managers.

Engineer Dr. Henry Damme who had the benign looks of a rosy-cheeked Norman Rockwell grandfather, was not only popular because of his powerful appearance. His enviable cerebral brain volume, combined with an engaging human forbearance, made him a cross between Albert Schweitzer and Benjamin Franklin.

In spite of his heavy schedule of meetings, the extremely busy Dr. Damme took time for everyone and everything. He always appeared like someone who takes time for five showers a day with time left over to mow his lawn, dry the dishes and listen to his favorite operas after office hours.

After several requests, I was finally granted an "audience" in Dr. Damme's office and made my way to his door like a son who is going to bargain with his father for a raise in his allowance. Bashfully, but with awkward cunning, I entered his office.

His disarming smile and endearing manners encouraged me to haggle for a degree of flexibility in my work schedule. I was able to extract his promise that I could begin my musical studies every workday between 12:30 and 4 p.m. This arrangement made me as happy as a bag lady who has just got a job as a bag boy at Publix.

It is true, I had to sit behind my drawing board one hour earlier than my colleagues at the P.T.T. to make up for the "lost time," but the idea and thoughts about sopranos who not only had lovely voices, but also were lovely to look at and . . . were allowed to be touched . . . stimulated me to arise every day as early as 6 a.m.

As a return service to the P.T.T., I had to promise my benefactor that I would follow up my four-year stint at the Conservatory by demonstrating my accomplishments in the form of a gratis concert in the large Congress Hall of the main P.T.T. building in Amsterdam.

I, indeed, did this and Dr. Damme sat proudly in the first row. I adored him, fully aware that without his indulgent foresight, I would probably still standing behind a drawing board, suppressing a talent that would have been stifled just as it was about to come to fulfillment.

Posthumously, I would like to send Dr. Damme a bouquet of flowers to heaven where he probably is a popular and beloved angel.

At the Conservatory, I also had lessons at night three times a week. Such a day looked like this:

6:00 a.m. — Out from under the feathers of my snug bed, dreading the impact of the chilling linoleum under the soles of my feet.

7:30 a.m. — Office check-in, on the way to my drawing pencil.

Noon — Released from the P.T.T. to pedal to the Conservatory, where for four hours I followed lessons in harmony, opera, literature and stage movement, singing, piano and foreign languages.

4:30 p.m. — Return to the frigidity of the drawing department to finish the pencil-lines that I had begun some nine hours before.

5:30 p.m. — Scramble to find my bicycle among several hundred others and wheel my way home through the forever chilly, wet Dutch climate to my mother's carefully prepared meal that I, in gluttonous ingratitude, guzzled down in my eagerness to satisfy an empty, tired body.

After this procedure, devoid of all table manners, I once again jumped onto my "wire donkey" and sped back to the barbaric benches of the Conservatory.

Three hours later, I was finally unleashed for the trek home with my head spinning in musical analysis and 101 melodies that refused to relinquish my worn-out brain cells.

Jam-packed and sometimes overflowing years but never to be forgotten.

I was extremely fortunate to have had Professor Dr. Lothar von Wallerstein as my teacher of the dramaturgical part of my opera studies. Dr. Wallerstein had determined that I was not, as generally thought, a baritone, but that my light high voice was definitely that of a tenor.

He was himself an enthusiastic actor and his numerous activities as a stage director had taken him to illustrious opera houses such as La Scala, London's Covent

Garden and the Metropolitan in New York City.

Wallerstein demonstrated every role for his students before the apprentice was invited to try to follow in the footsteps of the master. He taught us what it meant to bring life to a role to such a degree that the impersonation became a realistic part of one's own body. He taught us that life is an animation of the soul.

His interpretations were so enthusiastic, not to say fanatic, that he often went to the limits of his own physical strength in his efforts to make us aware of why a singing actor had to delve deep into his innermost soul in order to give a veracious personification of the role as intended by composer and librettist.

One ill-fated night, he went literally overboard in his endeavor and his theatrical blood almost turned fatal for him. The subject matter was the opera *Der Freischütz* (The Free Shooter) by Carl Maria von Weber, and this unrealistic treatment of a Teutonic legend was one of Wallerstein's pet subjects. The famous tenor aria in the first act, *Through the Forest*, that is sung by the forester Max, is an euphoric but preeminent illustration of what can happen if a hysterical creature like Max does not approach matters with a smile and a grain of salt.

Max is dreadfully upset that he, again, did not win first prize in the annual target shooting competition. Partaking of spirits of the alcoholic kind prior to the contest to improve his aim, had made him see several more targets than one normally would see without such assistance.

The result was no accident. Moreover, the fact that Max's girlfriend Agatha had witnessed him shooting holes in the sky was an almost unbearable humiliation for him and Voodoo Max almost fell prey to his own quick temper.

So, here we have a first-class hysterical character who would, at one time, certainly be a big shot at a distinguished pro-wrestling match, where smugness and personal arrogance set the tone for such competitions. Good composers and librettists know what to do with this kind of peevish creature, and so did Wallerstein.

As a hypersensitive man, he interpreted the role with such realistic furor that at the end of his "performance," he collapsed into unconsciousness, brought on by a sudden heart attack. He was immediately transported to the intensive care unit of the nearest hospital, where he had some weeks to meditate on his unrelenting lightmindedness.

Meditation promotes self-awareness, so after that memorable Monday in 1950, he never again indulged himself in self-destructive teaching. His wife, an American soprano, told me later that Dr. Wallerstein had had his birthday on that fateful day. Aware of the fact his bad heart condition would not allow him to live out the century, he gave himself the birthday present of playing once more, with all his unrestricted talent, the complex role of Max.

An extraordinary high price to pay for his own present! One year later, he died of cardiac arrest at the age of 70. I am very grateful to have been his student.

Chapter Fifteen

Madame Boulanger and *La vie Parisienne*

In spite of my not-too-excessive talent and contrary to my expectations, the studies at the music academy in The Hague went well. As early as one year later, I was selected by the Dean of Music and the college board to represent the Conservatory as an exchange student in Brussels and Paris.

Through these concerts, a general view was given about talent and work in the respective countries. Voice, memory and behavior worked to my advantage and audiences, as well as press, were not niggardly with their compliments.

I was so enchanted by the manifold charms of Paris that I decided to stay on and study a while longer in the city of Montmartre and Montparnasse. The Dean of the Dutch conservatory, a white-haired gentleman who accompanied his wayward student — in a safeguarding, fatherly way — would have loved to stay behind with me in the city of frivolity and light. However, before he returned home to "mother's kitchen," he advised me to take up studies with a certain Madame Nadia Boulanger on Boulevard Clichey.

I knew from my French lessons that the word *boulanger* meant *baker* and everything in association with food, in those young years, had my utmost attention. Little did I know that for four decades, speaking her name in artistic circles was almost like praying. What a woman! What an intellect!

Born in Paris in 1887, Nadia Boulanger was only 14 years old when she took up her music apprenticeship with the famous French composer, Gabriel Fauré. Her mode of living and intellectual conduct of life soon became the topic of the day in the artistic society around the turn of the century.

Illustrious personalities such as Diaghilew, Ravel, Stravinsky, later Aaron Copeland, Virgil Thompson and Igor Markewitch, were regular visitors to Nadia's home which she shared with her talented younger sister, Lili, between 1936 and 1962.

She conducted world-famous orchestras, such as the Royal Philharmonic of London, the Boston Symphony and the New York Philharmonic. It was incredible what Nadia could accomplish in one single day without getting nervous. She divided her student classes into groups of 10-12 persons, but no one was persuaded to be a silent member of such a group, on the contrary.

She gave every student a free hand to correct or to lead other students, and the result was a satisfying homogeneity, where everyone was willing to share knowledge with his or her partner. Nadia was outright brilliant in dividing up her day. Never was there a moment that was not utilized and economically accounted for.

From her, I learned the significance of Hamlet's phrase, *To be or not to be*, referring to the values of the life-span visit that is permitted to us on this, our planet.

Due to her international fame, Nadia was, of course, in good graces with governmental and aristocratic circles and was often invited to receptions and other official occasions. Typical for her, however, was that she never accepted these privileges for herself alone, but selected a student or two to accompany her and thus gave the student the opportunity to gather experience in different circles.

One summer night in 1951, the then president of France, Vincent Auriol, gave a reception with an accompanying gala dinner in the ostentatious halls of the Palais de Chaillot. The occasion was the state visit of a well-known president of a friendly black African nation. Everything was done to keep on good footing with those newly independent countries because one never knew when one day they might find a uranium mine in their backyard.

President Auriol had invited Madame Boulanger to bring a couple of her singing protégés to the gala. So, attired in a much-too-large rented tuxedo, I paid my respects to the building adjacent to the Eiffel Tower. A dazzling spectacle opened my lackluster eyes to a world of tax-consuming splendor.

Seemingly endless stairways lifted me up to the halls of enjoyment, expectation and — food. On every second step going up to the stuffy reception hall, a peacock-like Republican Guardsman was posted in a Gilbert-and-Sullivan uniform, while in the square outside the palace, some 100 uniformed men were acting in a military fashion, mounted on white horses that were sometimes not behaving in a very aristocratic manner.

I was immensely impressed by the pomp and circumstance that in no way harmonized with the shabby conservatory student struggling on a yearly grant of 300 guilders. With a certain nonchalance, I quickly decided not to be too fastidious and face the facts and — the caviar. It is true that we had to oblige the gathered company by singing some Orlando di Lasso and Händel works but, as a "service-in-return," we were permitted to join the illustrious crowd at the gluttony table after "everybody" had told "everybody" what they thought about "everybody."

That we were not only invited as decoration but also as escorts became evident as a distinguished-acting person in livery and white gloves showed me to table Number Three where I was planted next to a rather thin girl who, as I found out between the *hors d'oeuvres* and the soup, was the daughter of President Auriol.

How I deserved this honorable spot was not clear to me, but the needlepoint chair was comfortable and worth sitting on. Besides, my table partner was also alluring enough to ensnare my attention and was not only to be seen as an appetizer. Her name was Jacqueline and she turned out to be a charming, picturesque girl who tried to escape from the social track that, according to protocol, the president's daughter is supposed to ride.

She smoked incessantly as if to prove that one does not die of smoking in one single evening, and furthermore, she was not dressed in formal gala attire but showed her well-formed legs my means of a short, above the knee dress.

Between the stringbeans and a spoonful of caviar, she revealed to me that she, in her spare time, busied herself as an aviatrix, flying small sport-planes and that she, several times, had been on intimate footing with the "old man with the scythe" during unexpected emergency landings. However, it was clear as day that instead of going to the "happy hunting grounds," she became a frequent patient at various institutions for plastic surgery. Her disarmingly uncomplicated approach to things and her Mona Lisa smile during the "coffee with cognac" dance after the *créme caramel* was just the ticket for me.

We felt, instinctively, that our affinity to one another was mutual, which prompted Jacqueline to invite me the next day for a car drive through the *Bois-de-Boulogne* on condition that it was best to put a foot of distance between us during the trip.

Her motto was, "Be prepared!" The morning after the night before is oftentimes enlighteningly different, and after having bowed to my own pleasures, I was destined to play truant for a day from Nadia's valuable lessons. However, without much ado, Jacqueline entrusted to me the glad tidings that she had already twice nibbled at the apple of matrimony and that her desire for this kind of fruit had to be suppressed for the time being. Sorry about that, as Florida might have housed a former French president's son-in-law, if . . .

Two picture postcards was all I ever had from her after that, but by that time I was, myself, munching on apples from Eve's store. Out of obstinacy, I continued life in the fast lane by admiring the French wines more than I should have.

Although the Moulin Rouge and Tabarin were unreachable for my scanty finances, I discovered the possibility, via a waitress and the chief bouncer, to use the back doors of these establishments, which became a golden gate to me. The nights were frequently elongated into the wee morning hours and I often knocked about the streets of an awakening Paris, seeing the milkman on his way.

Rising those mornings was obviously a laborious necessity, not to speak of keeping up with the inestimable classes conducted by Mme. Boulanger.

What is sweet cannot last long. After six months of *La vie Parisienne*, I left the city on the Seine River with a wealth of wisdom for years to come and a totally empty wallet.

At Christmas 1972, I received a last farewell from an almost blind Nadia, saying that this Christmas card would be the last one that she would ever send, due to her failing eyesight.

Exemplary of her greatness was that she thanked us, her students and friends, that we had made it possible to fill her rich life, which she, through us and for us, had the possibilities to fulfill.

I have her Christmas relic as a grateful memory of a wonderful and distinguished human being.

Nadia Boulanger died in 1979, at the blessed age of 92.

Chapter Sixteen

Surviving the opening night's monkey business

After my six months of freebooting in frivolous Paree, it was a dull sacrifice for me to come to grips with the monotone day-by-day sound-drill of the conservative Conservatory of my hometown in The Hague.

Sunny student terraces like the ones of the *Quartier Latin* or picturesque alleyways in the *Montmartre* were not to be found in The Hague, let alone elegant receptions at palaces and other jolly establishments. No, the drums of the day were only beating out "study" and that was good, because my desire for learning had reached a critically low level after the licentious encounter with Paris and her easy seductions.

Many months passed by that were not worthy of being noticed, when finally the yellowish gleam of my musical aptitude dawned on the distant horizon. Even before I had completed my final examinations, I was able to start my stage career, however not in the provinces, as my orthodox teachers advised me to do. On the contrary!

Although it was only 1951 and the annihilating inferno of World War II was barely behind us, the performing arts, as they so often do in history, broke a lance for mutual reconciliation. The world-famous Vienna State Opera Company was to visit the Lowlands of Northwestern Europe on a reparation tour.

The opera that had been selected, *Der Rosenkavalier*, was the most popular work of the German-born composer Richard Strauss. Erich Kleiber had been chosen to conduct the performances. Lothar von Wallerstein was the stage director.

Strauss had been a well-liked "storefront" for the Nazis since 1933 and, like the Waldheims in our time, moved with the stream of events as long as was convenient. After the war, they assured the surviving world of their innocent obliviousness.

Conductor Erich Kleiber, like Strauss, born in the Germanic culture, was Jewish and a musical celebrity long before 1940. Following a scent of instinct, he had the presence of mind to flee his homeland and settled in Argentina. Lothar von Wallerstein, who was not an Aryan either, had been born of an aristocratic family in Vienna, but during those treacherous years had been hiding in Holland.

Both men were wise enough to recognize that forgiveness is far superior to vengeance, and resumed working with German and Austrian music companies for the praiseworthy cause of art and culture.

The main soprano role, that of the Marschallin, was interpreted by Anni Konetzny. She had the succulent appearance of the typical opera diva of the 19th century, when the voice of the performer was of utmost importance, while the looks were of little significance.

Anni measured a stately 6 foot, 2 inches on the yardstick and weighed in at a fine 220 pounds on the scales. Her Dolly Parton-like "balcony" had great quality but prevented an occasional glance at her shoes. Her voice, however, amply made up for all those imperfections.

Anni probably owed her 220 pounds to her famous colleague, Lotte Lehman who had sung from 1914 to 1939 at the Vienna and Berlin state opera houses. She fled from Nazi Germany just in time to find refuge in the USA. After 1945, she came to the aid of her former colleagues in far-off Vienna by sending them CARE packages of food. Lotte Lehman's humanitarian efforts were later honored by the Austrian government.

For the small but difficult role of the Italian Singer, a Dutch tenor by the name of Henk Noord had been engaged, much to everyone's surprise. He was a colossal

Surviving the opening night's monkey business

mountain of a man who, while his country was occupied by the enemy, sang in Berlin, the capital of the conquerors.

He had a rather lyrical voice, but due to his mighty physique, was "doomed" to sing heroic Wagner roles that were detrimental to his vocal cords and had ruined his once so beautiful voice. Deprived of an excessive quantity of brain power, his deteriorating voice did not prevent him from accepting the challenge of performing with some of the opera superstars of the time.

Aware that his "slip would be showing" should he sing during the rehearsals with full voice power, Noord was dexterous enough to mumble his way through, pretending that he had a slight cold. When the day of dress rehearsal had arrived, an aggravated Erich Kleiber burst his collar button in fury and demanded an explanation for Henk's stage mumble.

Knowing that he could not come up with a plausible justification, the tenor chose a dramatically irresponsible exit. A young baritone who was on stage with him at that moment, had to pay dearly for laughing at the situation in front of the irritated "voice producer." Worthy of Hulk Hogan, Henk Noord slowly and decisively walked up to the baritone, grabbed him under his arms and threw him like a sack of potatoes into the 6-foot deep orchestra pit where the timpani provided a safety net for him.

The pandemonium was complete. The tenor, now playing the role of an insulted, bloodthirsty liver sausage, promised anyone who dared come near him a cookie of the same dough! The baritone had to be transported to the hospital as several policemen who were summoned to the scene tried to tame the tenor, who proved once more the validity of the conjugation: "Stupid, More Stupid, Tenor!"

One day before the premiere, the task was to find somewhere another baritone and another tenor to save the performance. As the undertakers' slogan goes, "One man's death is another man's breath." Kleiber and Wallerstein made the decision to take two fresh, unspoiled "gems," of which I was one. I had two days to learn the part but young brains can achieve small wonders.

In the same opera, *Der Rosenkavalier*, there is also a small role called "the animal trader." The singer who sings this role carries a small animal on his shoulder, such as a parrot or a small dog, which he displays to an uninterested Marschallin.

The animal trader in our performances had a small but extremely jolly and lively monkey on his shoulder. During the opening night performance, while the Marschallin was having her hair touched up by her hairdresser and I, the Italian Singer, was busy singing my aria to her, I observed, from the corner of my left eye, that the monkey was trying to slip the collar over his head.

Unable to sing and shout at the same time, my "Watch it!" was only heard in my inner soul. I could only throw a glance of uttermost fright at the evidently unsuspecting animal trader who took my grimaces to be a particularly poor example of stage acting.

My fierce glance may have been noticed by the audience which did not know what to make of it, as it did not have anything to do with my role. Half-a-minute later, however, everybody understood my silent-movie acting, as the cunning monkey finally set himself free. With one tremendous leap, he took off from his master's shoulder and landed on the head and shoulders of a very startled Marschallin.

I kept on singing, almost subconsciously observing, to my delight, that the monkey snatched the glorious white powdered wig from the head of the prima donna as if he were picking coconuts in the African jungle. Aging approximately 20 years in 20 seconds, the soprano sat motionless with a dismayed glance in her eyes.

The actor-hairdresser who actually provoked the monkey's interest in the wig in the first place, had the presence of mind to cover the Marschallin's natural salt-and-pepper hair with a substitute wig. Hardly anyone noticed

Surviving the opening night's monkey business

this change of wigs, as the full attention of the audience was now drawn to the escapades of the monkey, with everybody puzzled as to what his next move would be.

With stylish hops, he leapt from box to box, generating shouts of hilarious laughter and jubilation throughout the first-nighter crowd of the sold-out house. The hubbub would take up to 15 minutes. Swinging his way from ground floor to stalls, hanging on to the gold lamé curtains and pulling wry faces, the monkey produced indignant sounds that could not be called savory.

The gleeful animal continued to wave the trophy headgear about like a cheerleader. Tarzan and Jane would have had a ball in the opera house that night. I could have sung, "For he is a jolly good fellow," or have taken off my trousers for that matter, but not one person, with the exception of the conductor, took notice of me anymore.

With some hastily procured monkey bread, the monkey show was finally stopped and the merry fellow was captured and put back into his monkey home. It must have been a gladiatorial feeling for Darwin's human model to gambol about in the elegant hall and be able to launch a scandal.

Later in my career, I sometimes had the same brigand feelings that that animal must have had. Let's monkey around and do something terribly hilarious. Or, for instance, when asked by the soprano during a performance of Mozart's *Magic Flute*, "Who are you?" simply say, "Charly Chaplin!"

Perhaps I have been too much of a coward to give the press a reason to write about anything else other than what they were supposed to write about. Maybe, one bold day, I will *do* it anyway, and maybe it will be in the south Florida Grand Opera House.

Chapter Seventeen

A shaky audition, and then the wait

Being the "new kid on the block" in an ocean of good-to-excellent talented opera singers is like trying to attract the attention of a professional football coach after having finished college. Forget it!

Loitering about on a street corner, waiting for the General Manager of the Metropolitan Opera to come to me and say, "Oh, that's where you are! We've been looking for you all over the place. Now — would you have time and would be interested in honoring us by making your opera debut at the Met?" Forget it!

Purchasing a German Alsatian guide-dog, a pair of dark glasses and a white cane, singing hymns of praise on a drafty square on foggy autumn days, might provoke charity but would get me, at best, in the vicinity of a Salvation Army shelter rather than in an opera house. Forget it!

Having heard that some singers made a career singing with a radio station, I decided to travel to the Radio City of The Netherlands, 27 miles east of Amsterdam. The town of Hilversum houses all the radio and television studios in the country, thereby centralizing and satisfying a great deal of Holland's entertainment needs.

This concentrated form of combining all electronic musical activities into one single town seems, at first glance, more suitable for a socialist country, rather than for an ancient kingdom like The Netherlands, but it has advantages for a small country.

Although the eight networks are heavily subsidized by federal funds, the system also gives private citizens the opportunity to financially support the network of their preference by becoming a member of the specific broadcast company. The more members a network has, the more hours per day it may transmit its programs through one of the five radio or three television networks.

Three hours in the morning of education and news programs and six hours of nightly entertainment programming is all that the Dutch television addict is offered.

On a sunny spring morning in 1948, I had a good idea — without the assistance of anyone else! I took a day off from my job at the P.T.T., bought a third-class train ticket and traveled the 66 miles from The Hague to Hilversum.

Having arrived in the city of 80,000 residents and not being able to afford a taxi, I walked a blind course until I finally saw the stone brick structure of a particular radio station that appealed to me. All networks in Holland are denominational, such as Catholic or Protestant, and are not affiliated with any political party.

When I was 17 years young, I had a puppy love for a Catholic girl who was so pretty that she was able to persuade me to take up studies in the Catholic branch of Christianity. Standing in front of the impressive radio building, I detected the initials KRO, which in Dutch stands for Catholic Radio Organization.

Still remembering how to cross myself properly, in case I should need it, I entered the marvelous marble hallway, nervous as a lizard. "I have come to make an audition, Sir," I informed the black-capped hall porter.

"Well," said the man in a friendly manner, "what about first putting that in writing like everybody else does?"

"But," I insisted, "I have come all the way from The Hague, and I don't have any vacation days left to come back a second time."

"Well, son, why don't you sit down there on that marble bench while I go and see what I can do for you," said the friendly "people-greeter," adjusting his cap and proceeding to shuffle off to look for a solution.

Several minutes later, he returned in the same slow-

A shaky audition, and then the wait

motion pace as when he had left me, announcing that, due to his personal insistence, a certain gentleman would take a moment to listen to my supplication.

The "certain gentleman" — as he told me many years later — had been employed at the KRO just two weeks earlier and I was his first applicant for an audition. He walked up to me with an emotionless, empty face and behaved as if he was just about to go through the four most challenging minutes of his life.

Following in his wake came a sauntering, pale-faced young man with an artistic hairdo, who turned out to be the pianist. He peeked around his boss like a shy child hiding behind his mother's apron.

After making our acquaintance in three-seconds, we walked in duck formation to the audition studio. I provided some information about myself and then, after one minute of total silence, the ordeal began.

I don't remember what or how I sang, but 15 minutes later I found myself, empty-headed, on my way back to the railroad station, feeling much like Noah must have felt in his 500-foot "canoe" sitting atop Mount Ararat after a deluge of 40 days.

Was that all? Was that worth the excitement of two sleepless nights, music and words continuously droned through my skull? The nightmare of maybe missing my cue, forgetting my lines, or developing a "frog" in my throat at the moment of paramount beauty was all behind me before I realized what had happened.

The "certain gentleman" had promised that I would soon hear from him. But as so often is the case, after a distressful month of watching the mail box, would I be able, with clammy hands and dry throat, to open the envelope that might change my destiny?

The letter did not say one word about the quality of my audition performance, but in dry and frigid prose invited me to sing a solo recital with piano accompaniment.

I still remember that forty dollar, 25-minute recital as if

it had been yesterday and not back in 1948. In those old radio days, programs were not pre-recorded on tape for later broadcast, as most concerts are today. Every performance was a live adventure with all the accompanying negative and positive connotations.

In anticipation of the day of execution, the tension of exhausting preparations had left deep traces in my frail constitution. And when I finally arrived in the cold, uninviting studio, my nostrils refused to pass oxygen and my cheeks trembled like a rabbit's mouth while eating a carrot.

To prevent myself from swooning away on the wings of song and knowing that 80 muscles must be set in motion to make speech or singing possible, I had to make use of a high barstool in the studio, such as the ones used by bass fiddle players in symphony orchestras.

With deadly tired legs and a head threatened by desiccation, I could only think of one thing: "Why was I doing this to myself when life offers so many avocations that are pleasant?"

Then suddenly, there was no turning back anymore, as a monotone voice reverberated through the studio walls with the gloomy countdown that only 30 seconds were separating me from the first transfer of my singing voice to a world of unprepared listeners. Without a warning, the green studio light turned red and escape was no longer possible.

I had the feeling that Christians must have had in Emperor Nero's arena, when facing the hungry lions in 79 A.D. The Christians of that time, however, were in a better position than I was, as they still had time to pray and... they also knew the outcome of their ordeal.

This was not granted to me, because the first introductory chords were only four bars long and that was just enough time to inhale some desperately needed air into my lungs. I must have had a despondent expression on my face, judging by the frequent smiles of encouragement that the experienced pianist granted me.

A shaky audition, and then the wait

Looking back so many years later, my radio debut must have turned out better than it felt at the time because up until recently I sang many concerts for that same KRO Radio Station.

I am still tired and weak-kneed during a radio performance, but now for other reasons. My nostrils expel less air and my cheeks shake only because Father Time has reshaped them. Sometimes, I feel like singing while sitting on a restaurant barstool waiting to be seated for a meal, because sitting on a barstool reminds me of the "good old times" when the days were young and body and soul crisp.

Photographic Section

When John was still "little Johnny" — with father, mother and brother, Cor, sporting a crew cut.

John (left), brother, Cor, and their dog, Wotan.

John, little sister, Greetje, and their late brother, Cor.

My very first tuxedo, at age 20.

Posing for a role in the Metro-Goldwyn movie, Betrayed. I made it!

Photographic Section

My very first leading role as "Marquis," in the French Opera, Les Cloches de Corneville, *1943.*

Still singing, 50 years later in 1993, as the "Messenger" in Aida.

In the startling production of the Fledermaus, *as "Prince Orlofsky," at the Amsterdam Opera House.*

In the title role as "the Count of Ory," in Rossini's opera of the same name, at the Berlin Opera House.

With the legendary Tito Gobbi, in Verdi's Falstaff, *at the Cologne Opera House.*

As *"Prince Sou-Chong," in Lehar's* Land of Smiles *during a television production in Vienna.*

Recording for Deutsche Grammophone of the Opera Palestrina, *with Swedish colleague Nicolai Gedda.*

With Bayreuth basses, Bernt Weikl and Walter Berry, during a television session in London.

With star soprano and friend Kiri Te Kanawa, at London's Sheperton Film Studio, shooting Figaro.

Recording Carmina Burana *for E.M.I., with Conductor Riccardo Muti and Composer Carl Orff.*

Eurovision Television Show in Amsterdam. The late Josephine Baker in conversation with Queen Beatrix, while I am telling the latest joke to Prince Claus of the Netherlands.

Paying a visit to vocal colleague from the other guild — Tony Bennett.

The night I was knighted by the hand of the Ambassador of the Netherlands

Photographic Section

As "Basilio" in Le Nozze Di Figaro, *at the Salzburg Festival, with Graziella Scutti and Dietrich Fischer-Dieskau.*

Recording session in Vienna, with friend and colleague, Hermann Prey.

With star Conductor Raphael Kubilik, during a concert tour in Switzerland.

Louise and I flank our legendary singing teacher, Vera Schwarz, who sang the world premier of Land of Smiles with Richard Tauber.

As the "Prompter" in Richard Strauss's Capriccio, at the Brussels Opera House.

Louise likes it! Vocalizing at the concert hall in Barcelona.

As "Nureddin" in The Barber of Bagdad, *by Peter Cornelius, at the (then) East-Berlin Opera House.*

Photographic Section

Meeting Queen Elisabeth of Belgium after my concert in Brussels.

With lovely Loni Andersen during a night on the town.

Concert at "La Scala" in Milano, with Zubin Metha as conductor.

Shooting the movie Carmina Burana at the Bavaria Studio in Munich, with friend — and one of the greatest composers of this century — Carl Orff.

As "Zephoris" in Adam's lyric opera, si j'etais Roi (King for a Day), at the Munich Opera House.

As "Marquis de Chateauneuf" in Zar and Zimmermann (Czar and Carpenter) at the Vienna Opera House.

In the role that gave me so much trouble, as "Harlequin" in Wolf-Ferrari Le Donne Curiose *(The Inquisitive Women).*

With Louise at our winter home in Munich.

With Louise and Sandy in our tulip garden in Munich.

In performance for "Help the Hungry at Home, Inc."

Photographic Section 123

John and volunteers buy, box and deliver food for the needy on a regular basis.

Appreciative recipients receiving food boxes . . .

The greatest day of my life. Louise has just said, "Yes!"

Chapter Eighteen

An untimely and a timely entrance to the opera *Don Giovanni*

My weekly appearances on Dutch radio programs not only offered me the opportunity to put into musical practice what I learned over the years, they also yielded an opening for my future as a professional singer.

Four years of blood, sweat and tears studying music and languages were endured because I never lost sight of my ultimate goal — to finally lay down that drawing pencil as soon as I could afford to do so, in exchange for a professional life on the stage that meant the world to me.

Thanks to several successful auditions for radio stations and concert agencies, at the right time and right place, my name became known in the right circles. Consequently, offers started pouring into the mail box. After some propitious recitals of classical music, I was asked to sing my first opera in a radio program similar to the popular Metropolitan-Texaco broadcast on Saturday afternoons.

Although I had never sung a complete opera role, I eagerly accepted the chance to sing for a large radio audience. The opera in question was Mozart's masterpiece, *Don Giovanni*, with its majestic overture and intriguing treatment.

The tenor role, that of Don Ottavio, is one of the most popular and sought after plums in the entire opera repertoire for tenors. So I was extremely lucky, again, to be able to sing that role for my debut.

The title role of *Don Giovanni* was sung by the legendary Italian bass, Cesare Siepi, who had sung the part numerous times before at the Met and La Scala. Like a supportive father to his son, he gave me a helping "lung" in how best to portray the difficult role.

Four strenuous days of rehearsing with piano and, later, with orchestra, singing endless repeats and modifications, gave the illustrious crew of soloists ample time to become acquainted with this particular radio performance.

The actual live broadcast, as it was written in my contract, was to be on a Sunday evening at 7:30 p.m. To give the singers a chance to rest their vocal cords, the conductor had decided not to have rehearsals on the day of the broadcast. Although I was nervous with anticipation, I did not get up before 9 a.m. that Sunday morning.

That was, however, the very limit of my patience. A long day of vocalizing-resting-vocalizing, walking around the block and becoming decidedly more nervous, vocalizing and more resting, lay ahead of me until curtain time at 7:30 p.m. At 2:30 p.m., I discovered that I had lost my voice somewhere during the course of the day. Also, I could not remember any of the music to be sung. It was about time to say my final farewell to this grueling profession.

To banish these disturbing thoughts, I decided to go to the movies. The "flicks" started at 3:00 p.m. and would, as usual take about 2+ hours. Afterward, I could face life again under the shower in my hotel and I would, fresh as a faded daisy, enter the radio studio 20 minutes before broadcast time.

That was what I thought!

The movie, unfortunately, was one of those tapeworm-like historical epics and it was a good 3½ nerve-wrecking hours before I saw the light of day once again. However, having been born as one of those matter-of-fact Dutchmen, I looked into the immediate future unfazed, except for the necessity of the shower.

Paying attention not to lose the little bit of breath that had sat idly in my lungs during the 3½-hour movie, slowly I walked the mile back to the hotel, showered, took a quick snack at the bar, assembled my music score and left for the studio, sufficiently in time to have some relaxing 10 minutes before the musical zero hour.

An untimely and a timely entrance...

That was what I thought!

As if in a hypnotic trance, I sauntered into the studio dressing room to find that my colleagues had not yet arrived. But as it was only 7:20 p.m., there were still 10 minutes to go.

That was what I thought!

Suddenly, the door to the dressing room flew open and my paprika-red-faced impresario stumbled in, looking some 10 years older than I remembered him from the day before. Seeing that he was rapidly approaching a heart attack, I gently invited him to sit down and relax.

As composed as could be under the circumstances, he asked me in a hoarse voice, "Where have you been?"

"Who, me?" I questioned innocently. "I went to the movies and had a great time. I am now relaxed and don't know why you are so upset."

"The time of 7:30 p.m., as given in your contract, is wrong and the broadcast has begun at 7 p.m.," he said, showing me a copy of the contract that I had signed seven months earlier.

I tried to form an answer but he grabbed my arm and began dragging me through the long and totally abandoned corridor to the studio, where the flashing red light proclaimed, "NO ENTRY — BROADCAST IN PROGRESS!" In violation of all rules, the impresario pushed open the door and, as if I were seeing it as an outsider, I saw the full orchestra, conductor and soloists, playing and singing their hearts out, memorializing good old Amadeus' masterwork.

Only now did I get some paprika-color in my own face and slowly, but intensively, I began to shake. The only one who could see my metamorphosis was the lackadaisical-looking conductor standing on his podium. With an commanding gesture, he summoned me to come closer as fast as my legs would let me do so, because 20 seconds later, I had to sing one of my many lines in the duet with the soprano.

I had "only" missed four pages of singing and the soprano had filled in half of them. After the broadcast, I made the flippant suggestions to transfer $7.50 to her bank account for having sung some of my notes, but my inconsiderate joking was not appreciated.

Only after showing my contract with the erroneous time for the starting of the concert could I explain my tardiness. However, the fact that I had the cheek to go to the movies was inexcusable in their opinion.

The next morning, I left Holland's radio city, Hilversum, with mixed feelings, immediately embarking on a concert tour through Germany's famous Rhineland. Passing through the mining town of Gelsenkirchen with its remarkably modern opera theater, I made up my still cobwebbed mind to pay tribute to that music temple.

To my great delight, I saw that they were giving *Don Giovanni* that night — the same opera that had just taken several years off my life, the very day before. The ticket price was easy on my wallet, so being curious how other singers would interpret the roles, I prepared myself for an enjoyable evening.

As the first act proceeded, I could not help hearing that the tenor on stage was becoming more hoarse with every bar he sang, due, obviously, to a sudden attack of laryngitis. The poor fellow struggled to fight it off, but to no avail. Sometimes a singer can survive half-an-hour of indisposition but the tenor of that performance was not so lucky.

Hardly had the intermission started when the manager of the opera house, dressed in a tuxedo, stepped in front of the just-lowered curtain to pay his respects to the audience and announced that due to the tenor's misfortune, intermission that night might take longer than usual.

With my adrenaline pumping ideas into my brain, I got up from my seat and darted through the "No admittance" door to the left of the theater, gaining entrance to the backstage area. I walked up to the still upset theater manager who was deep in conference about what to do to save the

An untimely and a timely entrance...

performance.

Knowing that the man had no other choice than to throw in the towel, I introduced myself and suggested that he call in another tenor.

"Whom?" asked the manager, slightly irritated.

"Me," came the response triumphantly from the depth of my vocal cords. I told them that I had never done the role of Don Ottavio on the stage but that I had sung the part the day before in a radio program in Holland. "You have no other alternative," said the conductor to the manager.

"A gift from heaven," said the manager sarcastically. But when I told him that I could only sing the part in Italian and not, like the rest of the cast in the German language, his jaw dropped several inches.

Taking the "musical bull by the horns," I suggested that the hoarse tenor should, for the rest of the performance, only act the role on stage and mime the text without actually singing. At the same time, I would *sing* the role from the orchestra pit.

The problem was that the tenor mimed the German text, while I sang in Italian and, of course, some lines were much shorter or longer in the other language.

"What destiny, oh, horrible burden," lamented the soprano in German on stage to her mute tenor. "*Cosa e stato?*"

I returned from the pit, "*Mio bene, fato coraggio!*"

"What does he want from her?" a perplexed person in the audience asked his wife.

It was a confusion of tongues in *optima forma* and the poor audience had to suffer through it. The Babel of Tongues improvisation, however, was the better of several evils, such as sending 1,200 ticket buyers to the box office to get their money back, for one.

In the end, my substituting for the tenor's voice was well received by the audience. Instead of the expected boos, we all got a long, standing ovation.

I took my bow standing on stage in street clothes between the singers dressed in their fancy costumes.

The manager and the conductor were pleased to such a degree that they offered me a contract, on the spot, to sing the same role the next season. In later years, I sang numerous times on the stage of Gelsenkirchen's opera house.

Although living in Tequesta now, I have maintained the friendship of a colleague whom I met on that very stage years ago in those turbulent times. It was Marilyn Horne, the world-famous American mezzo-soprano who at the age of 17(!) sang the role of Carmen Jones in the film of that name, for the actress Dorothy Dandridge.

Marilyn began her illustrious stage career in that dusty, coal-mining town of Gelsenkirchen in far-off Germany. Maybe, one lucky day, I will ask her to sing with me here, in our own Jupiter/Tequesta between her engagements at the Met and Italy's La Scala. Just for old times' sake.

Chapter Nineteen

How the beautiful, nearsighted singer made my day

Our beloved greatest grandparents, Adam and Eve, were pathetically poor because, since the time of his creation, Adam had been unemployed. Furthermore, he never attended school. To keep himself busy, he began breeding reptiles in his backyard, while Eve started an apple orchard whose juicy fruits nourished them during the long winter nights.

They couldn't afford a house so they lived like homeless people in our time, in the garden. The opportunity of complaining to the union did not arise until several million years later.

However, Adam (human being) and Eve (life) detecting the word "togetherness," looked meaningfully into one another's eyes and went to work on some snakebites and apples. Lo and behold, the unexpected happened. In due time, Eve bore a son whom they named Cain, which means "spear" in Hebrew.

After some more apples and snakebites, Adam knew all about Eve and a second boy joined the community. Having run out of ideas for names, they called him Abel, which only means "son" in Hebrew. They were a real happy family in their somewhat untidy orchard, which they had come to name "Paradise," as Adam remembered "paradise" means "park" in ancient Greek.

One day, while playing with his boys in the Mesopotamian sunshine, Adam showed them his great talent in rope-vine-swinging, while eating an apple at the same time. Brazen as he was, his carelessness played a trick on him. A bite of the apple went the wrong way and became stuck in his windpipe at the spot that we now know as "Adam's apple."

The stuck apple must have hurt because Adam began to utter cries, and we have to accept the scientific theory that those sounds were the first singing tones ever produced on our planet.

So, here we have finally arrived at the quintessential question of the mystery: what is singing? First, we have to endure the technical process. We open the mouth, take a deep breath and while exhaling, we let air pass through our vocal cords until a tone is generated.

Those tones we define as singing. If we simultaneously also say a word on this tone, the result can be much more effective. It would be splitting hairs to attempt to determine which was first, tone or word. In Richard Strauss' opera *Capriccio*, the tenor and the baritone squabble all night over which is more important, music or words.

Trying to find out if musical theater is more popular than the legitimate stage would be like asking a child, whom does he love more, daddy or mummy? Singing starts where speech cannot reach a higher power of expression and opera should, in its optimal structure, be an amalgam of poetry and music.

It is known that the Greek poet Homer sang his poems to the people rather than speaking them, as he felt that this would have a greater impact. This one-man show format has survived into our time, as I once experienced during my career.

The baroque elegance of the *Residenz Theater*, a legitimate stage in Munich, Germany, lends itself extremely well to the staging of the classical theater repertoire. Therefore, it did not surprise theater-minded Munichers when the manager announced in a press conference that he planned to produce during the next five years, five masterpieces by William Shakespeare.

The first production was *Othello* and for the second season, the semi-comical play *Twelfth Night* was selected.

How the beautiful, nearsighted singer made my day

This work, in which the comical side of the serious emotion of love is illustrated by the misadventures of two pairs or romantic lovers, needed much preparation and a carefully selected cast.

A renowned stage director in the Germanic theater world was selected to put the whole show on the road. Duke Orsino opens the play with these words: "If music be the food of love, play on; give me excess of it, that surfeiting, the appetite may sicken, and so die."

This line inspired the stage director to have a singing troubadour on stage, singing Elizabethan songs with lute accompaniment. I was chosen out of countless auditioners to sing John Dowland's 17th century songs.

While I was entertaining him with my singing, Duke Orsino was taking a bubble bath, lathered by an enormous, sponge-armed flunky. After I finished my warbling contribution, the still dripping Duke arose from his wet position, just as his love, Viola, entered the room. She walked up to her soppy, towel-covered paramour to kiss him passionately on his willing lips. Standing a few feet away from the scene of this ardent emotion, I was privileged to relish most of the wet ceremony.

After two weeks of flawless performances, the actress who portrayed Viola came down with the flu and had to cancel on the day of the show, creating a nightmare for the theater manager. He had, however, no time to mediate about his "maze," so the decision was taken at 4 p.m. to fly in a substitute Viola from Hamburg for the 7:30 p.m. performance.

A private airline came to the rescue, as well as police escorts through the cities of Hamburg and Munich, making it possible for the *locum tenens* Viola to arrive only 15 minutes before curtain time. Consequently, she had just enough time to dress in the borrowed costume and for the inevitable makeup. None of the other actors in the play had ever seen her before, but I can say from experience that it is not unusual for a guest performer, after having exchanged the first fiery kiss on stage, to whisper in his/her partner's ear, "My name is . . ." and continue the flow of proceedings.

After finishing my songs that evening, my role required that I help the servant wrap his serene dukeness in a towel, while looking in anticipation at the door, from whence the "fill-in" Viola was to make her entrance.

For a moment, standing in the blinding spotlight as if posing for Miss Universe, we had a fabulous view of what was to keep us busy and alert for the next three hours. An extremely beautiful example of Mother Nature, endowed with everything that raises a man's passion, dazzled our pupils.

Then, as prescribed by the stage director, she was to enter the scene and walk up to Duke Orsino with outspread arms and with lips ready for kissing. As if pulled by an elastic steel wire, our stage Viola walked, however, straight up to little me, bypassing Orsino as if he had leprosy.

To my utter delight and the jocundity of the Shakespeare crew on stage, she started at once her kissing ceremony on both sides of my eager face as if Jezebel had been her godmother.

Twittering from excitement and pretending to save the scene, I started, with extreme sneakiness, to take advantage of the offered opportunity. After I had given Viola ample time to say her first line, I reluctantly remembered that I did not have the slightest idea what Orsino had to answer, so I could not respond to her advances.

The real Orsino, in the meantime, had dried up enough to be able to walk toward us in his bath sheet and straw slippers. The pathetic bathroom appearance with the towel crossing over one shoulder contrasted strongly with the fantastic Elizabethan costume that I wore. Gently, he pulled Viola away from my unwilling arms and drew her to his own cheek while I watched the proceeding with dejected feelings.

Only during intermission was I told why I had been

How the beautiful, nearsighted singer made my day

treated so royally. In the excitement and due to the extremely short preparation time for her first appearance on stage, our substitute Viola had forgotten to put in her contact lenses. Being as nearsighted as a chicken, she just grabbed the first likely male figure within reach, thus being faithful to the Amazonian motto, "As long as it's a man, who cares?" and I became the object of her embraces. Her defense was, that in the Hamburg performance, Orsino is having breakfast, instead of taking a bubble bath, when she enters the room, but the explanation was too late to be of any use.

The knowledgeable audience that night could not understand what had made Viola kiss the pseudo secondhand minstrel first, before seeking the lips of his dukeship. We laughed a lot that night in Munich because Shakespeare is so sublime that even a mixed-up kissing scene cannot do harm to the greatness of *Twelfth Night*.

Humor is when one laughs in spite of . . .

Chapter Twenty

The teenage opera groupie who stalked my every move

To be in the public eye is not always honey, roses and raptures, especially for a performing artist. There are times and fans that would have been better off not to have existed at all, but many celebrities can protect their privacy, should they prefer to do so.

However, there are fans so totally devoted to one particular artist that their devotion almost turns into an addiction. Asked the question, "Why?" the widest variety of effusive assurances of "undying love" are displayed.

Often, these gushing melodramas are totally devoid of reality and have nothing to do with the art of the performer. There are any number of situations where the behavior of fans can turn an artist into a neurotic victim. Many television, movie and show personalities in the USA suffer in this respect. But in Europe, opera singers have to swallow the same sour vinegar.

Being tolerant with bullheaded admirers often encourages them to actions that can be truly unhinging. One lovely summer evening in July, I had successfully completed a performance of the Mozart opera *The Magic Flute* at the opera house in the Bavarian capital city of Munich. It was 11:30 p.m. and, after having changed my fancy theatrical stage personality into an ordinary "man about town," I complied with the request of fans to sign autographs at the stage door. Afterward, I meandered through the sultry evening air to a nearby taxi stand to go home.

Stopping at a display window, I observed a figure in the reflecting windowpane, standing some six feet directly behind me and giving me a stare that would have made

Buster Keaton green with envy.

"Hello," I said, turning around as neutrally as possible, to a girl obviously not more than 16 years old. "What is your name?"

A frozen gaze framed a deadly silence as only King Tut must have experienced in his tomb. Looking forward to my "after-performance" cigar at home, I just continued on my way to the taxi stand where, unfortunately, no taxis were available at that moment.

Accepting that misfortune, I decided to "take my legs under my arms" and walk the 30 minutes to my home, as the evening was balmy and I could use the exercise.

My wife, Louise, knowing that a dry throat is enemy No.1 for an opera singer, had packed some of my favorite Granny Smith apples into my briefcase before I had left home. Hardly had I sunk my teeth into an apple when I once more became aware of the feeling of being observed from behind.

Knowing that the backside of my body doesn't look any better than the front side, I whirled about with a mouth full of apple to find the girl, again looking at me with a dark haze in her eyes.

"Do you want my autograph?" I asked her and started to fumble in my briefcase for a pen. No reply.

"Would you like to have an apple?" I asked, producing the last of Louise's crop, thinking that forbidden fruit is sweet.

"*Nein*," came the answer finally, in a dark-brown Lucille Ball voice. I took one step forward, willing to show her some "*perestroika*," but she took to her heels like a scared cat. Had I perhaps eaten too much garlic with dinner that night?

Consuming the rest of my "Granny" on my way home, I had to smile at such innocent inexperience in the ways of the world. Little did I know!

Some weeks later, there was a repeat performance of Mozart's masterwork at the opera house and I was again invited to portray the tenor role of Tamino. It was a full moon that July night, as if to encourage all lunatics at large. The astrological sign of the zodiac displayed Cancer, with all attending circumstances to create a Dr. Jekyll and Mr. Hyde experience.

This time I had gone to the theater in my own car. After the performance, as I returned to the parking lot, I noticed from a distance that a package had been placed on the hood of my car. I picked up the object and looked around, hoping to see the person who had made this nice unexpected gesture, but no one was in sight.

The package was wrapped in white tissue paper and I could see the brand name of a well-known chocolate firm through the spotless white wrapping. Presuming that Zeus, the popular Greek god, could not have sent Pandora down again with her disease-laden box, I decided to eat the tempting contents of the package once I got into my car.

With the package in my hand, I proceeded to open the car door, when suddenly I felt a slight quivering inside the box. I impulsively reacted as if I had stepped with my bare feet on a slithering rattlesnake.

Jumping a foot high into the smooth evening air, I simultaneously threw the package away from me as far as I was able to. Back down on Mother Earth, I stood, rooted to the ground, staring with fixed eyes at the now atrocious object. Seconds dragged on like minutes in the expectation that the inevitable Apocalypse would be upon me. I stuck my fingers into my ears and squeezed my eyes shut, waiting for the big bang.

Suddenly, a ripping sound strained through the soft, spring evening. Relieved, I shuffled toward the box but was immediately struck by the odor that would have made all living skunks dance for joy. It was a stink bomb!

I could surmise who had placed it on my car, but I couldn't prove a thing. It was, however, an unpleasant, offensive experience.

Three months later, I went on a concert tour by train through the southern part of Italy. On that particular day I had my birthday, and as the train approached Naples, I felt somewhat lost and sad, knowing that no one could share with me this special day.

When I returned to my compartment from lunch in the dining car, humming "Happy Birthday" to myself, there was a package on the seat where I had been sitting earlier. I picked it up, but then immediately recalled the Munich incident. With a reflex action, I opened the window and threw the *corpus delicti* out onto Italy's sacred soil, as if it had been a rotten egg.

Once bitten, twice shy, said my inner voice. I explored the entire train to find "the girl" — with the exception of the "for ladies only" compartment — but without any result. That week, on tour through Italy's lovely region of Campania, I felt extremely uncomfortable, aware somehow that I was being observed from behind trees and on street corners, but I had to cope with it.

On the fourth day, there was an anonymous note for me at the hotel desk, written in German, saying, "I was sitting behind you yesterday when you visited St. Peter's Basilica."

I shuddered to think of what could have happened but had to reconcile myself to the fact that it could not have been avoided.

Not long after this Italian intermezzo, I was singing the rather lugubrious role of the astrologer in Rimsky-Korsakov's wonderful opera *The Golden Cockerel*, at the State Opera House in Munich. As instructed by the stage director, I walked slowly, eyes downcast, along a line of "village farmers," on my way to center stage, where I was to sing a glorious aria. Having arrived halfway, I unintentionally stopped as an uncanny feeling overcame me, sending shivers, like an electric shock, through my entire body.

Looking up from the shoes at which I had been staring, my eyes met the stone-cold face of "the girl," two feet away. She had not only managed to pass by the security guard of the theater, but she had convinced the wardrobe lady that

The teenage opera groupie who stalked my every move 141

she was new in the chorus and needed a costume.

Resisting the rather inartistic impulse to grab her in a stranglehold and yell, "Now I've gotcha!" I continued my seemingly endless journey to center stage, as if in a trance. What the . . . was that girl doing there on stage and what were her intentions?

After the performance, I suddenly knew what to do! Still in my astrologer's costume, complete with makeup and long white "Ho-Chi-Minh" beard, I raced downstairs to the artists' exit before the girl could possibly have had time to leave the theater.

I waited for about 30 minutes, like an 18-year-old on his first date. However, seeing all my snickering colleagues leave for home, I finally had enough of the masquerade. This was disparaging my honor!

Angry as a provoked spider, I ran back up the stairway to go to my dressing room. As I was crossing the now-empty stage, my steps faltered. Could she be hiding here, in the most Holy of Holies?

The iron fire curtain had already been lowered and only the uninviting glare of a night light shone forth, creating a weird atmosphere of emptiness.

Suddenly I heard a noise coming from behind some stage props. I ran toward the place where the sound had come from but still did not see "the girl." Almost inclined to throw in the towel and put an end to my whimsical private-eye excursion, I again heard the noise.

This time, I determined that it had come from behind an old stage set decorated with a landscape scene that had not been used for the past 10 operas. Somewhat vacillating, I pulled the canvas toward me as if an attacking raccoon might be hiding behind it.

Not a raccoon, not even a snake in the grass, but crouched in the corner, like an exhausted and frightened animal, was "the girl." She looked at me with impenetrably fearful eyes, waiting for the final death blow. I intended to tell her a thing or two that cannot be found in nursery rhymes, but seeing that hunched-up bundle of utter misery, commiseration befell me.

I stretched out my hand as in Michelangelo's *Creation*, to pull her from her precarious position.

"What is your name?" I demanded in a headmaster's tone of voice.

"Brigitta," she answered timorously.

With total determination, I took her roughly by the arm and marched her into the neighboring ladies' room and promptly locked the door. Then I proceeded to my dressing room to remove my makeup and to change from my "monkey suit" into a more respectable attire. Unlocking Brigitta from her temporary prison, I took her down the stairway and out the door, passing a very surprised-looking security guard who had just decided to close shop for the night.

I steered Brigitta to my parked car and sat her down next to me. She was silent as a mouse as I drove through the quiet streets to her parents' home address. The girl's mother opened the door, looked at us and shook her head despairingly.

"I knew that it would come to this," she said to her daughter, with a tear in her voice.

I did not have to introduce myself, as the girl's mother led me into Brigitta's room where pictures of me, in costume and in civilian clothes, decorated all the walls, as if the Beatles had not been at the peak of their popularity in those days.

"But she is 16 and I am 39," I said, in an effort to clear up the rather annoying situation. "Please sit down," the lady said and began to tell me the sad story of Brigitta's father who, at the youthful age of 26, had to give his life in the snow fields of Russia for Hitler's megalomaniac war, thus leaving a wife and a three-month-old offspring behind.

"She never had a father and you are the substitute," I was told. This explanation did not leave any room for defense. The words, "Madam, don't make me laugh!" were on the tip of my tongue. Should I accept the idealistic explanation of a loving mother, or not? — Still waters run deep.

Although Brigitta's superabundant adulation throughout those years was not a reason to send her to a corrections institution or a reform school, it was with relief when I learned that her mother had sent her off to boarding school near far-off Heidelberg, away from the temptation of theaters and tenors.

An artist's life is a privileged one, that is, until Brigitta will find out that I have moved to Tequesta.

Chapter Twenty-One

What did we ever do before television?

A stupendous phenomenon had made its entry into the living rooms of The Netherlands in the late 1940s — television. The first bashful steps toward that doomsday were made in 1936 by the giant Dutch electronics firm of Philips Light Bulbs and Radio Corp.
In cooperation with Germany's Telefunken and Hitler's propaganda ministry, Philips transmitted the Berlin Olympic Games of 1936 to 600 TV sets in Germany and 25 in The Netherlands. That electronic fanfare, however, never had a chance of surviving beyond the embryo stage in those prewar years, as Hitler, rejecting the advice of his propaganda chief, Josef Göbbels, preferred to put his money into bullets rather than television.
After Word War II, however, electronics corporations all over the world saw the great potential of the medium that would eventually rule our world and change our entire lives.
Consequently, Philips of The Netherlands rose to the occasion. In their infancy, broadcasts did not surpass the "Lilliputian" level for several years. However, by 1953 the time seemed ripe for some cultural adventure. The bold decision was made to produce an opera for the first time in the history of Dutch TV. Because little Mozart was only 12 years old when he composed his primogenial opera, *Bastien and Bastienne*, this work seemed an appropriate project to serve as the operatic guinea pig.
In spite the — by 1994 standards — rather inferior TV equipment, the telecast of Amadeus' uncomplicated, youthful musical undertaking went smoothly. As a result, my

humble name is imprinted in the archives of Dutch television as having participated in its first operatic production in Holland.

The German word for television is *Fernsehen* which means far-seeing. When we turn back the clock some 100 years, we discover the secret of the birth of this "far-seeing" mechanism.

The Polish-German-Russian inventor, Paul Gottlieb Nipkow, was a great admirer of the French brothers Lumière, who made themselves immortal by inventing the ingredients of cinematography during the second half of the 19th century. That made it possible for all of us to enjoy the "flicks."

I can imagine that the invention of what we now call television, went this way: Paul Nipkow had an aversion to leaving his home at night, so he began fiddling with some hypersensitive discs, which he perforated with small holes. When Mrs. Nipkow, on a foggy November night, anno 1884, went down to the cellar to see what her Paul was doing there for the past three months, he greeted her with these historic words: "Mother, put some bottles of cold beer and a bowl of popcorn next to my easy chair, because I think I have just invented the television!"

"Mother" found this statement unbelievable and returned to the kitchen to fluff up the potatoes.

After the evening meal, Paul returned to his do-it-yourself workshop, and while enjoying a cozy cup of after-dinner coffee, he experienced, on his new far-seeing machine the first earthly news item which stated that he, Paul Nipkow, had just invented the television!

For some of us, 100 years later, it is hard to imagine living one's life without television.

Before World War II, an evening at home went something like this: The day's work over, a pleasurable and long evening was enjoyed. Father told the family about the wiles and woes of his working day and the children confessed all disobedient acts at school.

What did we ever do before television?

After dinner, the valuable and instructive evening continued with the reading of books and newspapers, playing of games, or just conversing about one thing or another. Children helped their mothers and they, in turn, were helped by father with homework problems in math or science. If there really was nothing else to do, one wrote letters to relatives and friends, just putting thoughts to paper. Sometimes one would even take a walk around the block.

At 10:30 p.m., one was still so relaxed and satisfied from all those worthwhile occupations that it was a struggle to say farewell to the day and go to rest. What a wasted time it must must have been for our worthy ancestors before television was invented. We are far better off now that we do have television.

We no longer remain at the table after the meal is over, talking about "worthless" subjects, lest we miss the first "worthy" items of the TV evening. We have to judge the world events that we have brought upon ourselves. "Useless" talk is superfluous, as it is no one's concern what father has experienced that day at work.

Who is the mope who wants to know what the lads have learned about the worries of "new" countries in our complex world? Those countries are far away from my plate, anyway. No vain talk, but immediately after the last bite and with a mouthful of nourishment still remaining, we rush to the prime seat in front of the TV set and settle in for the rest of the evening.

Motto: "He who sits best, sees best." Quickly, we procure peanuts and popcorn, beer and cigarettes, preparing for the after-dinner evening gala on the tube, which can now take possession of us. We don't need to think anymore, because the box is going to do it for us. Just sit back and look, stare and gawk.

No more book reading if we want to keep up with the 40 million illiterates — statistics. No more math because we now have a calculator to do the counting for us. Let the Braves, the Red Sox, the Lakers and the soaps rule our lives. No more childish games, needles conversations of superfluous subjects. Just sit and stare 345 nights a year, enriching our spirits and broadening our outlook — just be looking.

That is 345 times three hours, which equals 1,035 hours per year in front of the tube, because we go away on a 20-day holiday when we don't look at television, or . . .? Altogether, our sitting and gawking comprises 130 days times eight hours. What about that?!

Around 9:30 p.m., the tension has become so intense that we slowly close the eyes in order to concentrate better. We let our head sink to our chest or we let it drop unto the back of our chair, whereupon our mouth drops open.

No, we are not away in the Land of Nod, but we are "concentrating" better in this manner. When we are finally roused from our dreams, we feel certain that we have gone through another evening of docility and enrichment. Our children and grandchildren will profit from our knowledge because we will be able to tell them everything that we have learned.

We will continue to raise children in the tradition and manner of TV culture, and if they listen carefully to us, they will, just like us, let the greatest vexation created by man pass over their souls. These offspring of ours, after a full life, will close their eyes in the certainty that they were better off than the generations of people who have lived before them — and before television.

Oh, blessed unwitting ancestors, why did we do it?! Father, forgive us for we know not what we do.

Chapter Twenty-Two

With Clark, Lana, Victor and Lex on location in Delft

Not being able to make financial ends meet in those early years as a singer, I had to accept all kinds of artistic jobs even when there were no notes to sing in the assignment.

One night, the telephone rang in my parental home and a male voice asked me if I was interested in money, excitement and fame. Also, had I ever been in motion pictures during my life on earth?

"Did you ever do any acting?" the man wanted to know.

"I don't do anything else in life, Sir," I answered capriciously. Many things had slipped my memory at that moment, but I clearly remembered that I had never been in the movies.

Being a great admirer of Hollywood's most dominating product — business, I thought that it wouldn't do any harm to pull some other tricks from my artistic stunt bag, other than just singing an opera or two.

"Great," said the man on the other end of the line, as if he had just made the catch of the day. "Tomorrow morning at 6 a.m., be at the old Market Square in picturesque Delft, just south of The Hague."

"Six o'clock," I gibbered, articulating in Shakespearean fashion.

"It's up to you," said the man, "take it or leave it. See you tomorrow!"

So, at 5:30 a.m. the next morning, I mounted my bicycle and sped off in the direction of Delft.

Arriving in the pottery town, hardly anything on the Market Square indicated a Hollywood production atmosphere. Crossing the cobblestone pavement, pushing my bicycle, I walked up to a man who was puttering about with some large spotlights.

I asked him if he was involved in the movie business. His dim, sleepy eyes looked at me from an unshaven face. He took the cigarette stub from his mouth and without saying a word, pointed to a girl sitting in the doorway of a restaurant that obviously had been open all night.

Seeing, that, to start a constructive conversation with this man would be more laborious than getting blood out of a stone, I decided that the girl in the opening of the doorway looked better anyway — at least from a distance. So my choice was easy.

I told the girl who I was and the reason for my presence in Delft. She promptly handed me a form on which I was to write my *curriculum vitae*.

"Just go inside, order some breakfast and wait for Mr. Reinhardt," she told me.

"Who is Mr. Reinhardt?" I inquired curiously.

"You either live behind the moon or you are just plain stupid," she said and did not pay any further attention to me. That I was given breakfast for just being present was something I welcomed as part of the many "goodies" that Hollywood had to offer to eager-to-learn youngsters.

At 7:30 a.m., while on my fifth glass of juice, a man tapped me on the shoulder and said, "I spoke with you yesterday on the phone. My name is Toonder and I am your agent for this movie, should they select your type. Come with me right away as Mr. Reinhardt wants to see you in his office."

Mr. Reinhardt, whose first name was Gottfried, was, as Mr. Toonder informed me, the son of the legendary stage and movie director Max Reinhardt. It was he who in 1920 founded the Salzburg Festival, now the most prominent festival in Europe.

Being Jewish, he had to flee the Nazis in the early 1930s, and went to Hollywood, where he directed his most heralded work, the film *A Midsummer Night's Dream* with the then 15-year-old Mickey Rooney as Puck.

Gottfried Reinhardt was not as illustrious as his father, but nevertheless, Metro-Goldwyn-Mayer had him under contract and he was now in Holland to direct the movie *Betrayed*. The story of this film is about a Dutch resistance fighter during World War II and was written about a living person whom I happened to know.

Gottfried Reinhardt was a convivial, chubby man with friendly blue eyes, which were fixed in examination upon me for a good two minutes, as if I was an antique piece at an auction.

"Would you like a small role in this movie?" he asked. He could have asked me if I would have liked strawberries with whipped cream. Both answers would have been identical — "Yes, Sir!"

"All right," the movie director said. "You're hired. I'll introduce you to Miss Turner if and when she gets here today."

In this day and age, Turner's first name is Ted from CNN, but in the 1950s, Turner was Lana, a small but extremely well-formed and beautiful young woman who was destined to be my playmate.

Mr. Toonder told me later that my other "partners" were Clark Gable, Victor Mature, Louis Calhern, Wilfrid Hyde-White and O.E. Hasse who played the role of the German Admiral Canaris.

Miss Turner was not as supercilious as I had feared her to be, however a healthy and clear distance between a greenhorn amateur and an arrived Hollywood star was firmly established from the first moment that I was allowed to touch her alabaster-like little white hand.

Victor Mature, however, was mature in name only, since his behavior was often rather im-Mature, when one considers his rank in the movie world. He possessed the remarkable talent of being able to produce a belch while speaking, or to speak while belching, whatever was convenient at that particular moment.

The eruptions were often so loud that the hundreds of pigeons nesting in the tower of the noble 13th century Grand Cathedral had to seek safety in flight when they felt insulted by the disgorging deportment of the famous screen star.

Mature frequently used his natural capabilities as a form of an alarm clock during the high noon siesta when the actors were taking their catnaps. The stately, centuries-old square resonated with the violent sound and I'm sure the many kings and queens of the Dutch Royal House of Orange-Nassau who have been entombed in the holy grounds of the Grand Cathedral since 1346 must have turned in their graves, half-frightened to death.

Clark Gable, on the other hand, was a debonair but introverted man who preferred holding "audiences" in his temporary mobile home rather than leave the trailer. *Gone With The Wind* already had a 15-year history, and this fact had put the stamp of aloofness on him.

However, in spite of his voluntary confinement, Gable was not without humor, especially when it came to pulling one of his practical jokes on an innocent victim.

A man, who actually was not a member of the cast, had also entered the scene early on and was, to some of the cast, a nuisance. Lex Barker later made a name for himself as an interpreter of Tarzan roles, thanks to his good looks and 6-foot, 4-inch frame. He was, however, so convinced of his irresistibility that it made him insufferable!

Being a natural philanderer, Barker would have made love to a cactus in an emergency. Moreover, he had a glib tongue that would have made him capable of selling a double bed to the pope.

The reason for his preposterous presence was Lana Turner, to whom he displayed his lust at the most improper moments. For an actor or an actress, making a motion picture means that 20 percent of the time one is working and 80 percent of the time waiting to be called up for that work.

With Clark, Lana, Victor and Lex on location in Delft

At last, Lex's advances which often came at very inopportune times had proved to be too much for Lana and she unburdened herself to Clark.

The "King" from Cadiz, Ohio, who had been in the movie business since 1928 and had won two Oscars for best actor, liked to take the liberty of indulging in an occasional practical joke. On a boring afternoon, while we were waiting for the sun to appear, Gable's jack-of-all-trades, Bob, told me that the "King" wanted to have a word with me in his trailer.

My self-esteem became so gilt-edged by this invitation, that upon entering his trailer I had forgotten Gable's name.

"Sit down, young fellow," he said in his congenial, charming way. "You're Dutch and probably know better what I am looking for. I have been troubled by an intestinal congestion during the past few days and would like you to get me a medication from the local pharmacy to unblock this evil."

He looked at me through the well-known squinting eyes, that had been constantly irritated over the years by strong camera lights.

For a moment, I had to translate in my mind what a "congested intestine" meant to a legendary movie star, since my knowledge of the English language at that time was not up to par on matters of physiology.

After some descriptive gesturing, the "King and I" finally understood each other.

"Please be discreet!" he suggested. I nodded assent and was as proud as a peacock to have been taken into confidence about the "internal affairs" of a man, who was the object of the dreams of 99 out of 100 women. He handed me a 10 *guilder* note and I stole away to the pharmacist like a thief in the night.

It was a child's play to find an effective remedy to improve the condition of Clark Gable's innermost feelings. As his courier, I hastily delivered the soothing drops that would restore the well-being of the movie star. An autographed picture was my reward.

The case of the blocked inner tube, for me, was closed. Not, however, for Mr. Gable who had been totally aggravated by Barker's swanky, sexual masculinity and his constant presence on the set. Finally, having brooded for some time over how to get rid of the troublemaker, Gable confided to Barker that he also knew what's what in the domain of conquering womenfolk. In fact, he said, he had secret drops to stimulate passion that would open all floodgates of the imagination.

Lex eagerly accepted the offered "elixir of love" that promised to enhance his great appetite for feminine beauty. Not being able to read the Dutch label on the bottle, Barker emptied one-third of the receptacle into a glass of water, swallowed the liquid and waited for ascension into Seventh Heaven.

The next morning, rumor had it that Lex Barker had been biding his time on the toilet seat in the bathroom twice that night, from 9 p.m. to 2 a.m. and from 3 a.m. to 8 a.m. Subsequently he was confined to his hotel room for the next five days.

Gable commiserated with Barker, suggesting that some mean little kid must have double-crossed him. Of course, Gable and I knew exactly who that "mean little kid" was and often, during the shooting of the movie, he shot appreciative and knowing looks in my direction.

The friendship between Lana, Clark and Lex suffered a temporary crack. Some time later, however, Lana did marry Lex — for a while, at least.

As Samuel Johnson once put it about 1780, "marriage has many pains but celibacy has no pleasures." I sincerely hope that my cooperation in this matter did not destroy any future conjunction among the stars.

After spending several hours a day in the solitude of the smallest relief room in his hotel, Lex finally had to leave for Germany to work on a film production.

I have no way of knowing whether the abdominal vicissitudes had worked to bring to an end his urgency of amorous pursuits. However, the experience with the products of Hollywood's dream factory is something that I shall never forget.

Chapter Twenty-Three

Tales of weak bladder, strong voice

My singing career had taken off and I was flying on the wings of song across God's musical fields, accepting every opportunity to stretch my vocal cords, to the delight of many a mortal music lover.

In those years, I sang the greatest variety of concerts before the microphones of Dutch radio stations, pleasing friends and relatives alike. One day, we performed a Mass by the Austrian composer Franz Joseph Haydn with the Radio Philharmonic Orchestra and its aging conductor, Albert van Raalte.

Mr. van Raalte, a kindhearted asparagus-like 6-foot-3-inch man, already had 90 percent of his 50-year career behind him. He enjoyed the privileges of people whose years are numbered, such as sitting on a high bar stool during his conducting exercises.

He seldom gave a soloist a cue, making it often a puzzle to figure out his gestures, whether he had indeed given a cue or had just run his hand over his completely bald head. After several days, we became immune to his gymnastics.

However, what annoyed us most were two human frailties in the maestro's daily life.

First, he was the proud owner of a set of rather discolored dentures, obviously due to smoking. This third set of teeth was a size too large so that often a rickety, rattling sound could be heard, accompanying the efforts of the orchestra.

Secondly, the maestro was burdened by the fact that he no longer was in full control of his bladder.

In the middle of the broadcast of Haydn's *Mass*, just as we had come to terms with the dental rhythms, Mr. van Raalte stepped down from the podium, walked up to the first violinist, whispered something in his ear and then went tippy-toe out of the studio.

To keep the musical train moving, the violinist, without missing a beat, continued Haydn's masterpiece using his bow as a baton. Some minutes later, the conductor returned to the studio, visibly relieved from his hardship. Beaming like a polished apple and walking much faster now than on his way out of the studio, he re-mounted the platform and commenced to wave his arms again.

The experience must have discomfited van Raalte to such a degree that he had forgotten his third set of teeth in the "powder room." Without a second thought, he spirited off once more, abandoning the *Benedictus* to its fate.

After two minutes, he was back a second time at home base and the *Agnus Dei* was a mere trifle. Below the belt, he was empty and above, he was filled up again. So, with patriarchal superiority, he attacked the remaining music bars.

The orchestra and the soloists were well acquainted with the weakness of his waterworks and generally forgave maestro. However, I have to admit that, up to this very day, I have never understood why van Raalte needed to remove his dentures while relieving himself.

Another famous conductor in those years was Maestro Paul van Kempen, disrespectfully baptized Kemp by the music clan. He was born in the Dutch university town of Leyden but had, what was inconceivable to me, a heavy German accent. This was most likely due to the fact that for several years, he had been the music director of the philharmonic orchestra of Dresden.

One "blue" Monday, I was engaged to sing the tenor part in a radio performance of Mozart's *Davidde Penitente*. Paul van Kempen was the conductor. In my complacency, the easy-appearing music of the master from Salzburg seemed an effortless task. So, in my overconfidence, I did not even open the score until I entered the radio studio for the first time. Three days before the actual live performance, we had the first rehearsal and, to my surprise, I was blundering so intolerably that Maestro van Kempen began to curse and swear at me — in accentfree Dutch.

He was so angry that he broke his baton in two and left the studio in wild Toscanini-fashion. Although I was sweating carrots and onions, I had not managed to master Mozart's masterwork from sight, as I thought I could. I had the suspicion that Amadeus had played an unfair trick on me but I could not complain to him anymore.

When the well-tempered "Kemp" returned to the studio, I had to admit remorsefully that I evidently had less talent than was generally supposed. I tried to pacify the maestro and production manager Manus Williamsen by saying that I had the entire weekend ahead of me to learn the part.

However, what I did not disclose was that I had to sing two additional concerts in Belgium that same weekend! Having to drive the car to Belgium and be there for rehearsals and concerts would make it impossible for me to even take the time to look over the score of *Davidde Penitente*.

Desperate to find a solution, I told the producer that I had signed a contract in Antwerp. But after he had recovered his breath, I assured him that I would immediately return after the Antwerp concert and would drive through the night to his home in Utrecht (Holland), where I would spend the night. The plan was approved.

I was, indeed, at 2 a.m., the morning of that Monday on the doorstep of a yawning Manus, who opened the door with the obviously paramount question: "Do you know your music?" I was too sleepy to go into a discussion and answered with some dexterity: "What do you think?!"

He showed me to the guestroom and when I was alone, I took the music score from my suitcase for the first time since our abortive rehearsal, three days earlier. Five minutes later, my eyes refused to stay open any longer. I had just time to place the music score under my pillow before trailing off into dreamland.

After what seemed only a few minutes later, I was startled in my sleep as Manus' slap shocked me out of the cozy arms of Morpheus, telling me that it was 8 a.m. and that in two hours, we had to be at the studio in Hilversum, 25 miles away.

I recovered the score from under my pillow and, exactly at 10 a.m., fresh as a one-month-old carton of milk, I stood in front of the all-revealing microphone. Deadly tired and with a blinding headache, I was convinced that my short but rising radio career would come to a premature end that day.

Not knowing one note more or better than three days before, I proceeded to sing at my first cue, shaking like an aspen leaf, convinced that I was about to dishonor myself forever before the entire orchestra, choir and singing colleagues.

However, the inexplicable happened! As I sang on without making one error, Maestro van Kempen smiled benignly at me from his cockpit, stopped the rehearsal, stepped down from the podium and advanced toward me. While kissing me on both cheeks, he said in his mixed Dutch-German: *"See, mein boy, ich knew that du would not disappoint me."*

At the broadcast that same night, I must have lost several pounds of much needed body substance, but every note was in the right place where good ole' Mozart had written it. I never told anyone about my "pillow technique" and duly request my readers not to let it get around.

On that radio day in Holland, I learned that concentration and a little praying was of more value than talent or knowledge. For an Indian guru, a welcome working field, and for a New York psychiatrist, five hours on the couch.

Chapter Twenty-Four

The spirit of the dead composer played on

In this crucial time of ethnic warfare in the former Yugoslavia, with its peoples fighting for their national identity, I am reminded of a sensitive period in my life that relates to this scenic Balkan republic.

It was the summer of 1958 when I decided to journey to Austria for some badly needed coaching and also, to have my vocal cords "oiled and relined" at Salzburg's music educational temple, the Mozarteum.

Apart from the internationally famous annual music and drama festival, the Mozarteum is the most prestigious institution of this town of 130,000 souls. It carries the name of Salzburg's greatest son, Wolfgang Amadeus Mozart.

For the advanced musician, the Mozarteum is, in the summer season, a deliverance from the artistic daily routine. It offers a concentrated six-week study course given in all facets of music by some of the most prominent teachers to be found on the European continent.

I took up opera study and acting classes, as well as vocal lessons from a fascinating woman named Vera Schwarz. In her prime years, Vera Schwarz had been one of the most celebrated dramatic sopranos of the European opera stage.

Born in what later became Yugoslavia, she perceived the light of day at a time in history when the state of Croatia, where her cradle stood, was part of the Austro-Hungarian Empire. Very conscious of her patriotic heritage, Vera Schwarz never considered herself a Yugoslav but always a proud Croat.

Another Croat, born eight years earlier in the same

city of Zagreb, was a fellow by the name of Josip Broz. At the outbreak of World War I, he was conscripted into the Austrian army, and was captured and taken a POW by the Czarist Russian army. He was freed in 1917, following the Russian revolution.

During World War II, Broz became the leader of the Yugoslav resistance movement against the Nazi occupation of their country, using the pseudonym "Tito."

Vera and Tito had both attended the same high school in Zagreb and the charismatic Tito had fallen head over heels in love with the attractive and very temperamental Vera. In 1923, he became the leader of the Yugoslav Metal Workers Union and tried to snare the lovely Vera for the feminist movement, hoping to take advantage of her outgoing personality to promote his own agenda.

Vera, much more interested in using her vocal cords to sing, rather than to scream political slogans, abandoned a likely future as Mme. Tito and first lady of Yugoslavia in favor of a life of passionate dedication to the Muses.

In a candid moment, Vera revealed to me that she had had several meetings with Marshal Tito but that, for the good of the country, both had finally decided that life was difficult enough trying to contain eight Slavic states as a united Yugoslavia without complicating it with a scandalous love affair.

Ironically, Tito had, later in the 1950s, a close relationship with another Croatian-born artist, the Metropolitan Opera soprano Zinka Milanov. Tito's wife, Jovanka, however, promised him that she would make mincemeat out of Milanov should he but once give in to the tender overtures of the sensational soprano.

During her illustrious singing years, Vera Schwarz's most frequent partner was the legendary Austrian tenor Richard Tauber, with whom she had performed regularly on the opera stages of Europe. In 1925, at the tender age of 26, at the request of Hungarian operetta composer Franz Lehár, Vera took a sabbatical from her 42 leading operatic

The spirit of the dead composer played on

roles to join Tauber, at the Berlin premiere of the operetta, *The Land of Smiles*.

This occasion marked the emergence of a formidable team in the singing world. Lehár, at the zenith of his artistic creativity, and Vera, with her temperament and charisma, were a worthy match for superstar Richard Tauber.

In 1933, the rising dangers of Germany's Nazism forced Tauber to emigrate to England. His amazing career ended abruptly in 1948 at the youthful age of 56 with his untimely death in London.

It was now 1958 and Vera had hung her vocal cords on the "coat rack" in exchange for the much sought-after teaching job at the Mozarteum in Salzburg. Being her favorite student, as Vera once told me, did not make it any easier for me to deal with her temper, as the combination of her milk-glass white skin and piercing steel-blue eyes had a coercive effect on her students.

One Sunday morning, Vera called me to tell me that that day was particularly troublesome for her as it marked the 10th anniversary of Tauber's death and also that of Lehár, who had died the same year but just one month after Tauber. Would I observe that memorable day with her by driving her to the southern Austrian town of Bad Ischl, where Lehár had lived and worked, and where his majestic villa is still a place of pilgrimage for operetta lovers?

I would and did. When we finally arrived at the front steps of the substantial building on the Traun River, I rang the doorbell. The vibrating cowbell sound inside the mansion brought back memories of bygone years when one did not push electric doorbells but pulled on cords in order to get the attention of the inhabitants.

When finally the gate did open, a tawny, white-haired gentleman, with sideburns reminiscent of the late Emperor Franz Josef who had spent his summers in Bad Ischl, appeared on the threshold. It was the same "Man Friday" butler who once served Franz Lehár for 35 years.

"Dear Madame," the man said courtly while stepping

back a respectful distance. "What joy overcomes me!"

As in the glory days of his master's life, he stepped to one side, deferring to the moment of evoking old memories. Without looking at him, Vera stretched out her arm and entered the huge chandeliered hallway that had been so familiar to her some 30 years before.

"I am back, Johann," she said firmly, "and I do remember the way to the study."

Straight as a proud peacock, she strode ceremoniously past the butler and began to ascend the long staircase to the great drawing room where the sofas, fauteuils and monumental paintings on the walls gave evidence of days of departed glory. Tottering in Vera's wake like two tugboats in a raging waterway, Johann and I looked smilingly but with appreciation of the situation, at each other.

"Hello," I said, trying to brighten up the solemn situation and just to say something to prove that I was not mute. Johann nodded his head in my direction and mumbled back an unintelligible salutation.

Having arrived at the top of the staircase, all three of us were out of breath, and this was not just because of the many steps or our advanced years.

"Sit down, John!" Vera said to me, still somewhat breathless, as she pointed to a round table covered with a white lace cloth and surrounded by four palatial chairs fit for the gods. I did what was commanded. Vera, seating herself next to me, gestured to Johann to place himself on the third chair.

After this formality, a silence as solemn as an owl floated through the plush-laden salon. I looked at Johann, expecting some oracular language. Perhaps the ceremonial seance of a table lifting off, or the mystical playing on the piano of a Lehár melody by unseen hands, but nothing happened.

When Vera at last broke the silence, she told us that on that very Sunday, 30 years earlier, she had been sitting around the same table, with Richard Tauber seated on the same chair where I humbly rested and Franz Lehár on the seat now occupied by Johann. In a dignified tone, Vera revealed to us that the illustrious triumvirate had signed the contracts for the world premiere of Lehár's great operetta, *The Land of Smiles*, which was later performed 250 times at the legendary Metropole Theater in Berlin.

As destiny so often surprises us, some years later, by sheer coincidence, I had my first permanent opera engagement with the very same theater, although in the meantime it had been renamed the Opera Comique of East Berlin. In spite of her advanced age, Vera traveled from Vienna to Berlin to be at my premiere in the theater that was so close to her heart.

Two years later, I received a telephone call from a well-known Viennese soprano. She informed me that Vera had not long to live and that she had expressed the wish to see me and my wife, Louise, one final time.

Forsaken by her many fans of old, and not having ever been married or having any living relative, Vera had elected to finish her earthly journey in the same town, Bad Ischl, where her beloved master, Franz Lehár had also departed this life.

That very same day, Louise and I traveled the 180 miles from Munich to the Lehár capital and found Vera desolate and at the limit of her energy.

When the head nurse informed Vera of our arrival at the hospital, we were requested to wait in the long, dismal corridor outside her room. In trying to recapture and preserve memories of bygone times, Vera had asked the nurse to provide her with cosmetics so as to improve the color of her sallow skin.

The steel-blue eyes that had once demanded so much respect were still radiant but were only a reflection of their erstwhile beauty. The dark shadow of death was already playing upon her transitory features. Her smile was still proud but the once-so-noble voice was only a pale echo of departed glory.

"Hold my hand, John," she whispered and I recognized the desire for spiritual comfort that was ready to leave pride behind. Our conservation was limited to gazing at each other but our parallel thoughts were drawn to an all-embracing beyond, into Parnassus where we would find our reward.

The next morning, Louise and I decided to return to the hospital for the last Good-bye, only to hear from the head nurse that Vera, a few hours after our visit the night before, had closed her pulchritudinous eyes forever. According to her last wish, she was interred at the same burial place where her idol, Franz Lehár, had been laid to rest.

Whenever I sing Viennese operetta music, I always remember Vera Schwarz with the steel-blue, mesmerizing eyes and feel gratitude for the privilege of having known her.

Chapter Twenty-Five

My surprise singing partner before the DAR

I did not know much about the patriotic women's society, Daughters of the American Revolution, when I was asked to add some luster to the commemoration of the 75th anniversary of this distinguished ladies club. To grace the occasion, the DAR board had decided that (a) the festive event should take place in an historically acclaimed location and (b) a person from an historically renowned country should be a soloist in the musical part of the program.

For the first item on the agenda, the exceptional Empire Room of the venerable Waldorf-Astoria Hotel in midtown Manhattan was chosen, but the second point of the agenda was less easy to solve.

The Pilgrim fathers numbered some 100 independent English Congregationalists when they boarded the *Mayflower* in 1620, preparing to flee England and its religious persecution. Some of them, however, made a port of call in The Netherlands and that fact was a charming delay, according to the DAR board.

Evidently, that little country in Northwestern Europe, with its wooden shoes, windmills, tulips and Peter Stuyvesant had enough historical clout, because my agent from Columbia Artists asked me if I would be interested in lending my vocal cords to reinforce the friendship between The Netherlands and the Daughters.

I have to admit that most of the Daughters were rather at the grandmother stage of life, but the party did not suffer a bit because of that small irregularity. I accepted their financially healthy offer with anticipation and traveled to the city on the Hudson River, where I was officially welcomed by the club's president, Mrs. Gloria Kellogg, who held audience in her townhouse on Park Avenue.

No corn flakes for lunch, but instead, a smile from ear to ear, laying bare a set of dentures worth at least $7,000. Her silvery purple-white hair and friendly steel-blue eyes behind the silver-rimmed glasses gave the semblance of grace and competence.

Although she handed me a voucher for a three-night stay at the Waldorf, Mrs. Kellogg inquired, in a motherly tone of voice, if a $1,000 advance fee would satisfy my requirements for earthly goods. Unabashed, I accepted the token of prosperity, knowing that my desires were greater than Mrs. Kellogg's needs. After the audience was terminated, I was sent on my way by a gloved butler, who even opened the front door for me.

Pausing several seconds on the front steps of Mrs. Kellogg's mansion, hoping that a friend or acquaintance might see me coming out of that doorway, my hopes quickly faded into banal triteness.

I promptly took a taxi to the hotel and a feeling of boundless exclusivity came over me as I commanded the driver "To the Waldorf please and don't spare the horses!" When the doorman of the luxurious lodging lifted his headgear and said formally, "Good day, Sir!" I knew that I could now die in peace, since I had obviously reached the paramount goal in life.

The bellboy at the hotel, who had left the boyhood stage behind him long ago, carried my suitcase to Suite 1626. When I, with a Humphrey Bogart gesture, tossed him a quarter, he remarked, without so much as a bat of an eyelid, "Good gracious, Sir, thank you! Finally I will be able to send my kids to college."

After his discontented departure, I first set my frame down in a huge armchair in which, according to the man at the reception desk, the king of Siam had sat, albeit in 1931. However, the king and I had little else in common. After I had opened and relished the satisfying sensualities of the

My surprise singing partner before the DAR

products that certain perfume manufacturers had scattered about the bathroom, I nestled down between the silky bed sheets and slept a beautifying sleep.

The next morning. I had a music rehearsal in the Empire Room of the hotel, together with the pianist and a female vocalist, as my impresario had put it. The pianist was no Vladimir Horowitz, but that was in keeping with my own capacities, as I was no Pavarotti, either, weighing in at only 160 pounds.

Knowing that our musical contribution would not find a place in the book of historical performances, we had to be content with the Olympic exhortation that taking part can be more gratifying than victory.

The Empire Room of the Waldorf is a replica of the grand drawing room of mad King Ludwig's fairy castle in the Bavarian Alps. It had colossal crystal chandeliers, huge silver candelabras and majestically imposing flower arrangements that, like an embellishing emerald, contrasted with the cobalt-blue of the floor covering. My mouth dropped open in such astonishment that a dentist would have been extremely satisfied.

While I let the superabundance of splendor pass before my eager pupils, an extremely elegant black woman floated gradually into the empty room. As a fierce adherent of aesthetics, I have to admit that exotic women have always awakened a certain semblance of sex-appeal in me, but this exclusive specimen of feminine beauty surpassed, by far, any expectations.

Without obvious movement of her legs under a long dress, she glided slowly toward us and with accommodating spirit, stretched out her roly-poly chocolate-colored arm and whispered softy, "Hi, boys!" Much to my delight, that plural salutation had also included my humble personality.

Just as I had inhaled some needed oxygen and prepared to launch an impressive sentence into the Waldorf atmosphere, the pianist answered with unsurpassed lassitude, "Hi, Pearl."

As a spark of lightning, it flashed through my perceptive sensorium that the mocha beauty who stood so palpably before me, was none other than the world famous soul and blues singer Pearl Bailey. I quickly snatched the hand that still dangled in front of me, realizing that one has to strike while the iron's hot.

For a moment, the narrow-minded temptation crossed my squalid brain to bite her hand as a token of internal fervor, but my perverse thoughts were called to order just in time to assume my natural graciousness.

Pearl said that she was one of us in the endeavor to satisfy the DAR ladies in their urge for culture. To some degree, I wondered, having been told that the Daughters and colored skin went together like salmon and peanut butter.

However, since the color of hatred is yellow and not brown, the Daughters had jumped the chromatic spectrum, knowing that regardless of her color, Pearl as a human being stood head and shoulders over onerous theories.

"What shall we do tomorrow?" she asked with a pleasant amiability. Clearly, the thought of "doing something" with Pearl made me choke with excitement. So, as the unrestrained, profligate joker that I am, I answered by asking if she could sing the duet from Bizet's opera, the *Pearl Fishers*.

Recognizing that behind my formal attire a naughty jester slumbered in me, Pearl gave a big smile, showing a marvelous set of teeth. After some cross-country guessing through the field of soloists' repertoire, we agreed ultimately on *Deep River*, the only spiritual that I knew.

I sang the song as deep as my high tenor voice was able to manage but it was more like fishing in troubled waters than in deep rivers. After some bars of tormented warbling, however, Pearl started to knit a melodious web of vocal "babadibas" and "bubalabubs."

It was formidable that all of a sudden what first sounded like a hoarse goat, as far as my part was con-

My surprise singing partner before the DAR

cerned, had become music. Just as we had decided to repeat our concoction, a huge black man entered the scene and, without saying a word, wrenched "my" Pearl from my side, like a red currant from the bush. I was suddenly left staring into space like a Haitian who sees snow for the first time in his life.

As a result of this abandonment, we were forced to face the consequences of our unpreparedness the next day. That night, as the gala was in full swing, and everyone had told herself and others how good they were, the then-mayor of New York City, John Lindsay, took the stand.

With his boyish Hollywood face — slender, handsome and intelligent — he had the DAR girls lying in a swoon at his feet, just like adoring teenagers. He was standing behind a lectern on the same floor level with the ladies. A glass of water in front of him and his manuscript on the pulpit gave the mayor the aura of a clergyman.

In the middle of his speech, the mayor, with great pathos and poignancy, spelled out in plain English how long the DAR's 75 years of existence had been.

To give his statement a kind of Italian explicitness, he stretched his arms wide open. In the path of this Corcovado posture, like a perfectly timed stage gesture, was a glass of water standing precisely in the line of fire. Gracefully arcing across the air, the full glass flew into the lap of a distinguished prudish-looking lady in the second row, with a splashingly wet result.

At a political or labor union convention, a stunt like this would have created shouts of joy from the opposition party, but the arsenic-and-old-lace ladies uttered cries that would have pierced a musician to the very bone marrow. A lovely-looking lady with a fruit basket for a hat on her purple head, sitting next to the victim, was shocked by the accident to such a degree that she predicted in a firm tone, to a timid-looking Lindsay, just exactly what would happen to the mayor in the next election.

Grumbling loudly, she accompanied the wet lady out

of the hall to help her change into a less soggy attire. The sniggering John Lindsay could not hold back the remark, "I'm glad that she's not my mother-in-law."

After 10 minutes, the now dry ladies returned to their seats and although the momentary mood had sunk below water level and looked more like an antique auction, jolly John had enough roguish witticisms up his sleeve to turn the evening again into one of festive mirth.

When Pearl and I finally trotted out into the ring, we had to pay the price for having had only one short "bubalabub" rehearsal for our duet. In spite of fierce attempts to come alongside with me, my partner could not repeat her performance of the day before and was in danger of listing to one side.

Confidently listening to my own voice so as not to lose the line of melody, I witnessed the heroic battle that Pearl fought to balance her "bubalabubs" at the correct time, in the exact place. Although our collision was cataclysmic, I had to admit that she went down with flying colors, while her slightly demolished stature, irritated by a whiff of whiskey, stood like a lighthouse in a November storm.

The Waldorf concert has taught me that it is possible to snatch victory out of the jaws of defeat, if a performer has the talent to touch upon the tender strings with a lot of "bubalabubs."

As a Dutchman, it was my good fortune to make the acquaintance of a privileged new world and of a country where potentials are still unlimited. Little did I know that some 20 years later, I would call that country home. God bless America.

Chapter Twenty-Six

Herbert, The Great

The superstar conductor Herbert von Karajan invited me to join him and his Berlin Philharmonic Orchestra for an extended concert tour in Japan in commemoration of the anniversary of the dropping of the first atomic bomb on an inhabited city. For occasions like this, Ludwig van Beethoven was expected, as usual to carry the Flag of Brotherhood with his war-horse and masterpiece, the *Ninth Symphony*, as well as the glorious *Missa Solemnis*.

Coming from the tiny kingdom of The Netherlands, I had been asked to represent Western Europe in the company of such star colleagues as Gundula Janowitz from Austria, Togo Nagano from Japan and the Finnish bass Martii Talvela.

Von Karajan labored with the hard working Japanese chorus as if they were preparing for a world championship bout. Ninety-five percent of the chorus members spoke only Japanese, so the maestro employed a phonetic method, working with groups of six or eight singers at a time.

With the Latin words of the *Missa*, this procedure worked to some extent, but when it came to the "Ode to Joy," the choral finale of Beethoven's last symphony with the lyrics of Friedrich von Schiller, Germany's greatest dramatist, the maestro was hard to please. Despite the indefatigable efforts of the Nipponese to sing *Alle Menschen werden Brüder* (All men will one day be brethren) without an accent, proved for them to be just as hard as singing *Hito wa mina Kyomdai ni Narimasy* would be for us. (The reader just has to believe me that this is how Schiller's words are rendered in Japanese.)

All concerts were great successes and the maestro was immensely pleased. That made a world of difference with this capricious superstar.

Von Karajan was difficult when in a good mood, so one can imagine what he was like when he had gotten out of the wrong side of the bed. It was all but impossible to have a word with him about anything having to do with music, let alone engaging him in a trivial personal conversation. One day, however, I managed to draw him into a dialogue.

I knew that it was von Karajan's habit to relax in his private dressing room during intermission of rehearsals. For approximately ten days in Tokyo, I had been waiting for a moment like this to bring him greetings from a mutual friend in Europe.

Nothing ventured, nothing gained . . . Fortune favors the bold . . . With some apprehension, I knocked on his dressing room door, but there was no response.

Only the weak would give up easily. So, in my youthful presumptuousness, I opened the door and peeked around the corner. Not seeing anybody, I did not want to press my luck and thought it wiser to sound the retreat before the general attacked. Just as I was in the process of closing the door ever so softly, I heard a voice saying in German, "Who is there?" No mistake about it, it was the voice of the genius of Salzburg.

Von Karajan had an unpleasant sounding, squeaky voice and talked so rapidly that it always seemed as if he were in a great hurry. Recognizing the voice was one thing, but I couldn't determine where it came from. I now had closed the door behind me and stood in the room, waiting for things to come.

I cleared my throat and answered timidly, "It's me, Maestro, van Kesteren."

One could always expect the unexpected with him, so my expectations were pitched high. After a few unruffled seconds, my waiting was rewarded.

Herbert, The Great

Alongside the wall stood a couch-settee that could be used to comfort exhausted maestros and, eventually, also for other activities. Slowly, the silver-gray curly head of His Eminence, von Karajan appeared from underneath the couch, as an auto mechanic would emerge from under a car after searching for oil leaks.

Looking down at him and seeing him for the first time in a horizontal position, I asked him in as casual and friendly a manner as I was able to, if I could be of any service.

Looking up at me, he remained where he was and explained in a business-like way that this Japanese dressing room did not have any drapes and the only way to concentrate and enjoy a moment of tranquillity was to crawl into the darkness under the sofa that stood 12 inches above the floor. It was a plausible explanation in my opinion.

Having said this, he retracted his famous head like a startled turtle and was out of my field of vision again. Staring at the now empty space in front of the couch, I felt like a pizza delivery boy must feel when his potential customer doesn't open the door.

What to do now? Mindful of the memorable words uttered by the famous French Marshal Ferdinand Foch during a desperate military situation, "My center is giving way, my right is in retreat; situation excellent, I shall attack," I decided that heavy artillery was my only salvation.

Without any further introduction, I now announced the greeting from the mutual friend and waited for a reaction. Ten seconds passed in anticipatory silence before a youthful-acting and supple Herbert von Karajan rolled out of his hiding place.

Knowing that for many years he had had a severely deformed spine which gave him a lot of pain and crippled him in his later years, I was very surprised to see how this sprightly man in his early sixties, measuring five feet and four inches and weighing only 104 pounds, made an extra effort to brush up his tough image for me. His sudden briskness, however, was not surprising. Our mutual friend whose name I invoked was a remarkably beautiful woman and the maestro was known to be attracted to feminine glamour.

He invited me to sit next to him on the couch and we started chatting away as if we were having a drink on a café terrace in Paris. All traces of the arrogance and ugliness for which he was so notorious, had suddenly disappeared. We found a mutual non-musical topic in a beautiful woman — something perfectly normal for any healthy man, as women are the spice of life.

This turned out to be the only personal conversation that I was privileged to have with Herbert von Karajan in the 24 years that I was to sing under his baton.

Chapter Twenty-Seven

Ill fortune seldom comes alone

After my vocal successes in the Land of the Rising Sun, conductor Herbert von Karajan invited me to sing with him in many countries around the world. Especially memorable was his request that I sing the tenor part with the Berlin Philharmonic Orchestra in the very first German performance of the *War Requiem* by the distinguished British composer Benjamin Britten.

This monumental work had its world premiere one year before in Coventry, in the south of England, whose cathedral and much of the town were totally destroyed in a World War Two air raid by the Nazi *Luftwaffe* in November 1942.

My partners in this eminently important cultural event were the Viennese soprano Wilma Lipp and the German baritone Dietrich Fischer-Dieskau. I looked forward with great anticipation to this historical concert, but I had totally failed to take into account the utterly unpredictable behavior of the devil, or just plain bad luck.

Two nights before the first rehearsal, I had a concert on the Berlin radio network S.F.B. with soprano Hilde Güden and bass Eberhard Wächter. After the concert we went to a popular restaurant in town to wash down the musical mistakes that we had been making that night.

I ordered a marinated leg of lamb with red cabbage, apple sauce and very tiny potatoes named *Pommes Noisettes*. I swigged down the affair with a deliciously tempered *Bordeaux* and the world seemed to have improved that night compared with earlier in the day.

But not for long!

After a delightful evening of wine, women and song,

we parted company well in the wee hours of the morning and retired to our respective hotels. I was in high spirits, unaware of the fact that Mephisto, the devil incarnate, was waiting for me in my hotel room, ready to procure me a night never to be forgotten.

At 1:30 in the morning, I pulled the sheets over my face but just as my head was about to touch the pillow, the magical hand of Mephisto turned the entire room upside down. I became dizzy to such a degree that I felt as if I was hanging, head down, from a trapeze.

I presumed that the excellent *Bordeaux* had pulled a practical joke on me, so I took a sleeping pill to get some rest before the rehearsal the next morning. That was the worst thing I could have done.

Around 3 a.m., I staggered out of bed, too sick to think clearly. Slowly, I waddled toward a window, intending to let in some fresh air but, like a crashing tree, I fell flat on my face. In no time at all, the expensive floor covering was strewn with remains of lamb, red cabbage, *Pommes Noisettes* and other tidbits beyond recognition.

Neglecting my disorderly conduct, I managed to crawl to the telephone and asked the front desk to immediately send for a doctor. Ten seconds later, I fell into a coma that would keep me unconscious for many hours.

As I was to learn later, the physician had come quickly and, with the help of the hotel staff, put me back in my bed. In my state of suspended animation, he could only guess about my malady but, after testing my blood and other bodily fluids, he did not need to be a medical genius to diagnose a severe case of food poisoning which, in some cases, could be fatal.

Around seven o'clock in the morning, I regained consciousness and perceived for the first time, with blurred vision, the outline of the man who had just saved my life. I felt needles in my arms and saw bottles with liquid hanging over my head, and realized that something was not kosher with this tenor. I was not up to starting a conversation, so I submitted passively and let him pump out what had remained in my stomach.

When the doctor noticed that my eyes once again began to focus on my surroundings, he told me that I was a very lucky man to be able to write one happy day about my dreadful experience. He advised me to stay in bed for a week or so, and take a ten-day vacation after that.

"Ha-Ha," roared Mephisto soundlessly. I smiled vaguely and would have loved to follow the doctor's advice, but for a small obstacle that could not be overlooked — the *War Requiem* concert that I, even at the cost of my health, was determined to sing.

When the doctor finally left after some seven hours at my bedside, I pulled myself together and called the management of the Berlin Philharmonic and told them that due to a mild case of indigestion, they have to do the first rehearsal the next day without me. I assured them that I would be fit as a fiddle for the following day.

The philharmonic folks were not amused but promised me with a trembling voice that they would inform Mæstro von Karajan, the Unmerciful. I had gained one day to spend between the sheets of my sickbed but the weakness from the fever and the headache kept me from sleeping one wink that night, while the dizziness made me feel as if I were sitting on a nonstop merry-go-round.

The doctor arrived again in the morning and announced that I had a 104 degree fever, which was not something to be sneezed at. I was, indeed, a very sick and stubborn opera singer. Later that day, I called the Philharmonic again and they wisely connected me with Mr. Top Manager himself.

Dr. Wolfgang Stresemann, a feared potentate, was the son of the brilliant post-World War One German politician, Chancellor Gustav Stresemann who received the Nobel Peace Prize in 1926. In a belligerent tone, Wolfgang Stresemann expounded on the phone, "Impossible, Mæstro von Karajan declared that your last chance is tomorrow, or else . . ."

Von Karajan had never conducted the colossal work before and therefore needed all the time he could find to practice with the orchestra and the singers. But then, I hadn't sung the part before either and I didn't even have a voice to fit at that moment. I also knew that with the Britten work being rather new, only one or two other tenors in the world had studied the part, which served to undergird my tenacity.

As cheerfully as my relaxed vocal cords allowed me, I said, "I promise to be there tomorrow morning." But this did not go across at all.

"I'll be at your hotel in 30 minutes and you will sign a Yes or No statement," promised Stresemann forcefully "and I will bring the Mæstro's personal secretary and counselor André Mattoni with me."

That put me on the horns of a dilemma: Did I go through this ordeal only to surrender in sight of the harbor, or would I have to face the music? "Perseverance brings in the game," I remembered and, weak and dehydrated, I called for the chambermaid to make the bed and tidy up the room for the first time in three days.

Looking in the bathroom mirror, I perceived an unsavory, ashen, feverish and unshaven visage that desperately needed a thorough restoration. My mother used to say that slicked back hair and a snazzy smelling aftershave could work wonders, so I followed her post-humous advice.

Just as the chambermaid was trying to rid the musty room of the smell of rotten bananas and apple cores, there came a knock at the door. Clad in my pajamas and morning gown, I could barely muster a bow for Dr. Stresemann and Mattoni.

Both gentlemen over-extended themselves with solicitousness but it was unclear to me whether it concerned my well-being, or was it due to the unease over the rapidly approaching concert date. I must have looked like a soggy floor mop but made a brave attempt to give the impression of being in roaring good health.

My transparent bluff concerning my state of health sent Mattoni in a rage and he promised, using some expletives, that I would never sing again with the Berlin Philharmonic if I fail to attend the dress rehearsal the next morning.

While the first wrinkles were building up in the elderly Mattoni's face that had the appearance of the skin of an overripe peach, Dr. Stresemann had his "I'll make you pay for this" look in his steel-blue Prussian eyes. In a voice of uttermost conviction I tried to assure them that I would definitely be at the rehearsal the next day — the only remaining rehearsal before the concert, and a crucial one because I had never before sung the part.

Knowing that they had no other choice than either me or no concert at all, they promised to return at five o'clock that afternoon to observe my recovery and to soothe their wounded pride.

These were no empty words because promptly and 17:00 hours, "Abbott and Costello" entered my room again, bringing a fruit basket full of goodies and a message from the Mæstro that he expected to see me the next morning. They were pleased to see that I, at last, was wearing a suit, but I had to cut their visit short because my bathroom was beckoning me for a guest appearance.

Five minutes after the two emissaries had gone, I nestled myself dead tired between the sheets and, for the first time, my subconscious warned me that I had probably gambled too high, especially because I did not feel any better than the day before.

Around seven o'clock I took again two sleeping pills and slept the unhealthy sleep of an addict until I woke up at eight the next morning. I felt a shade better and took an almost ice-cold shower, dressed myself in a manner befitting the importance of the day and went down to the breakfast room, ate some biscuit, then grabbed a taxi and arrived on time to appear on the stage of the Philharmonic Hall at 10 a.m. sharp.

I fully expected that the world-renowned and notoriously difficult von Karajan would reduce me to dust for having let him do all the preliminary work for the past several days and showing up only for harvesting the results.

I was way off the mark! The Mæstro appeared to be totally in control of his temper. As if he had not even noticed my absence for three days, he looked down at me from his conductor's podium and remarked in his unadulterated Salzburg dialect, "You lost weight! You're OK?"

I replied that I couldn't wait to start singing, upon which von Karajan exclaimed, *Also packe mer's* — meaning, "Then let's roll up our sleeves and start working!"

The rehearsal went smoothly, although the extreme concentration combined with frailty had drenched me in perspiration.

The concert that night was a grandiose event. Metaphysical vigor had given me the strength to do more than I could have expected myself to do. Could it be that there is indeed something that helps us when we cannot help ourselves any more?

Who knows?

Chapter Twenty-Eight

What secrets lay in the message from Andrei Gromyko?

When I made my second concert tour through the Soviet Union, I had an encounter that kept me busy for a long time afterward. The concerts that I performed were financed by the foreign exchange program of the Ministry of Culture and Education of the Federal Republic of Germany. When West Germany found it useful to expose itself in a propitious sunlight, the pocket book of the Bonn government was not avaricious.

Although the cultural piggybank was not as abundant as that of neighboring Austria where the national budget for culture is larger than that for national defense (Oh, blessed Empire!) — and for a long time cannon fodder was imperative for German culture — one must sleep in the bed one makes. In presenting itself to the outside world, however, the Federal Republic spent more money on caviar and champagne (the German call it *sekt*), than one can consume in a single dinner session.

It was not surprising, therefore, that after my performance in the Moscow Philharmonic Hall, a swank reception was thrown at the German Embassy, where we were given a warm welcome by the highly polished ambassador and his charming wife.

While enjoying sensual morsels that one seldom comes across at Salvation Army parties, and inundated with (alcoholic) potables that often collide with gluttony, one spoke with total strangers about topics that were as insignificant as the people who rattled them off.

The time span of such receptions is usually too short to make sophisticated impressions on your counterpart, but again, too long to keep the frame of mind at an intelligent level. Although *"ferrum alcoholisahun"* was originally a finely powdered iron, gradually the word became "essence," and Paracelsus defined it in the 16th century as "the most subtle part of anything." *"Alcool vini,"* as he called it, has had, since the Neanderthal age, an idiosyncratic effect on anyone who calls himself *Homo Sapiens*. The Arabic word for alcohol means "a pure conscience." That may be so, but when wine is in the man, wisdom is in the can!

While the ambassador entertained me with significant stories about this, that and other things, a sort of small man honored us with his presence, sipping like a proficient tippler at a glass of champagne and keeping extremely silent.

Whatever the reason, the slurping midget standing in front of us, could not create a favorable impression since silent party guests are like flees in a carpet — they are there but it is hard to get rid of them. I happen to belong to a race of people that prefers to know who is standing on the other side of their glass.

After some time, several other mortals tried to enlarge the existing circle but none of them made an impact on my left brain where the ability of recognition resides.

Having lived in Munich for many years, I acquired a Bavarian accent when speaking German. Therefore, when one of the champagne-sippers presumed that my cradle must have stood alongside the Isar River in the Bavarian metropolis, I cleared the air by making it public that my juvenile years were passed on the beaches of the seaside resort of Scheveningen. This resort is on the outskirts of my hometown, The Hague. And when I was building sand castles on the beach, the ladies were still wearing bathing suits from the Adam's apple to the kneecap.

"How come you have been sent on this goodwill tour if you don't possess German citizenship?" came the incredulous, interrogational question from the Ambassador.

The Waldheim syndrome suddenly awakened in me

and I thought, "*Thou also wast with Hitler of Braunau, for thy speech betrayeth thee.*"

Rousing from memories of the evil past, I said, "Well, as a performing artist, you don't need to pay attention to what country you compete for," trying to steer clear of the rocks. "But of greater importance is the financial security of one's concert fee."

At last the short man moved the champagne chalice from his lips and spoke in a nasal tone of voice: "But I happen to know that singers exclusively from the Federal Republic were invited to this benevolence tour."

"Well," I said, somewhat irritated since I knew that he was correct, "I once metamorphosed myself into being of the Jewish faith to make possible a concert appearance for myself at a synagogue, so why would I be shy about pretending to be of the German 'faith'?"

Now the German ambassador came into the harness, and finally introduced the small man to me as Mr. Bahr, the special envoy for the cabinet of then German Chancellor, Willy Brandt. Egon Bahr was in Moscow to reason with Leonid Brezhnev on several delicate points concerning world affairs.

Mr. Bahr, who, as I learned later, was half-Jewish and had escaped the Nazi camps by the skin of his teeth, riveted his split-pea-shaped eyes on me, trying to overcome his gap of eight inches between us. Having read about his subtle sarcastic remarks before the German Parliament, I prepared myself for a shower of remarkable remarks.

At that very moment, a person with a kind of wry appearance, whose surly face for over 40 years dominated the diplomatic world, stole his way into the circle.

The Ambassador, now somewhat disquieted, introduced Mr. Andrei Gromyko to me. Without looking me in the eye, he stretched out a slothful, pale hand in my direction.

This man had always been enigmatic to me since he took office in 1939 and counselor of the Soviet Embassy in Washington and then later as the Soviet Ambassador to the United States during World War II. He seemed to be timeless in his dark suit, vest and colorless necktie, while obviously knowing the secret of how never to laugh or be friendly in company.

That evening, "Mr. Nyet," as he was called in diplomatic circles, again looked immensely sour at my rosy "cheese head," probably thinking, "If we could just have more Dutch cheese in the U.S.S.R."

"Mr. Gromyko told me," chattered Egon Bahr suddenly, "that he has a soft spot in his heart for The Netherlanders because they fought so valiantly and took on such a noteworthy role during the Nazi occupation of their country."

This turn of babble gave an unexpected piquancy to the conversation, as we were on German soil, being in the German Embassy. I accepted the proffered praise for my countrymen, and thanked Egon Bahr for his triangular compliment.

To give testimony that he was able to speak, Andrei Gromyko asked me in smug English, "How is Mr. Luns? I have not seen him for a long time!"

Joseph Luns at the time was Secretary General of NATO in Europe and, because of that, the most weighty political figure in that North Atlantic "negotiating club." I knew Mr. Luns from the time that I hosted my own personality show on television in Holland, where I interviewed popular Dutch men and women. They mostly talked about themselves and that was the "hobby horse" of Holland's favorite political figure at that time, who always spoke in a colorful, stocky-affected accent.

Joseph Luns was not only 6 feet 5 inches tall, but he was also extremely Catholic and an eternal conservative right-winger, as far as his political and ideological spectrum was concerned. As a former Dutch foreign minister for eight years, he had, moreover, a disarming political sense of humor and it must have been torture for him to negotiate with the immensely humorless, diehard Stalinist from Moscow.

What secrets lay in the message from Andrei Gromyko?

"I don't know," I answered Mr. Gromyko truthfully, "I haven't seen Mr. Luns for a long time, either."

Now, the unmoving Andrei shuffled two steps closer to me and I expected some indoctrination to come directly from the top shelf. "Should you ever meet him again in the near future, please give him my sincere greetings, and tell him that the soup is not eaten as hot as it is served!"

I looked dumbfounded at Egon Bahr, hoping to get some explanatory assistance for the culinary statement, but Egon had returned to his old routine of champagne slurping.

I just commenced to chat about some ingredients for the soup and asked if Andrei was talking about pea soup, onion soup or borscht. However, the political signboard of the "evil empire" had already lost all interest in me and, without so much as a farewell kiss, Gromyko withdrew from the circle and with a sauntering gait, juice glass in hand, left to forage in other diplomatic fields.

"I thought they called this 'taking French leave,'" said one of the other party clowns in the circle, with a fine feel for timing. "That still must be Napoleon's phantom from 1812."

At that point, Egon Bahr held his finger to his lips, as if to conjure up Bonaparte's ghost.

Some time later, after having left the bustle of the cocktail party and seated in an embassy car going to my hotel, a strong desire to contribute to a better world understanding awoke in me.

Upon returning to The Netherlands, I informed the Foreign Office in The Hague about the delicate message that rested secretly in my bosom, which was meant for NATO chief Joseph Luns.

"So sorry, sir, the NATO headquarters are now in Brussels, Belgium," came the answer.

With the soup message still throbbing in my temples, I arrived back at my home in Munich where, shortly thereafter, I was invited to give a live radio interview about the musical happenings that ruled my life. I, however, turned the cultural program into a sham when, to the discontent of the radio host, I announced that I had a culinary message with secret ciphering, that might be crucial to the world.

"Can you tell us roughly what it is about?" asked the reporter guilefully, so as not to lose all.

I hesitated but could hardly say that the dispatch had something to do with hot soup, so I preferred to remain mysteriously silent.

To my dissatisfaction, the ensuing weeks brought no response from Washington, Brussels or London, and I was overcome with fear that St. John's Revelations in the New Testament were to be fulfilled and the Apocalypse of damnation was coming upon us if I did not deliver my "soup" message in time.

Driven to despair and harassed into thinking that NATO headquarters was just another phony KGB office, I passed my days in apathetic lethargy.

Then one day in 1985, dawn broke on the tormenting uncertainty about the soup. Tucked away in a little corner of an English bookstore in the old section of The Hague, I spotted the 6-foot 5-inch Secretary General with his moth-eaten mustache, turning over the leaves of precious old books. Sitting on a remarkably uncomfortable *tabouret*, the weighty man was deeply absorbed in his avocation. It was now or never for me!

Picking up another 12-inch-high *tabouret*, I placed myself directly next to him, which fact went completely unnoticed. To give the situation a more "undercover man" nuance, I whispered without looking at him who I was and that I could offer him a soup message from Moscow. With his Eden hat perched on his fairly large head, Mr. Luns looked somewhat loftily over his half-rimmed glasses at me and said, "Sorry, did you say something?"

Little did I know that NATO's top man was hard of hearing. Aware that a surprise delivery of my spy code was now a thing of the past, I repeated my line that "The soup is not eaten as hot as it is served."

"Amusing, very amusing, ha, ha." reflected Mr. Luns the feelings of his inner soul. "Sorry, but I am now retired and don't live in Brussels anymore, and Mr. Gromyko has recently been upgraded by Mr. Gorbachev to president of the U.S.S.R."

Fourteen months of impetuous heartburn and irksome nervous twitches came to a brusque ending, and I felt like a just-punctured balloon must have felt. Immensely disappointed by the sobriety in which my spy dream had ended, I made my parting "curtsy." In the meantime, Mr. Luns had already lost himself once again in the books of a distant past.

Departed glory! Maybe the world would have looked better today, had I been able to get my exposition all the way to Brussels. But, I was too busy singing in those years!

Chapter Twenty-Nine

Despite my agony, the show went on

During a Munich performance of Franz Joseph Haydn's opera, *The World on the Moon*, composed in 1777, something happened that was not written in the libretto.

The Czechoslovak stage director Buhomil Herlishka thought it a cute idea to change the original action from a "garden" on the moon, to a "circus" on the moon. Such liberties are not necessarily noble, but they are artistically permitted and globally accepted.

I was singing the part of the romantically tender-hearted Leandro, but was dressed as a harlequinesque *Punch and Judy* figure with large pom-poms down the front of my white silk buffonesque costume. A white painted face and a black clerical coif on a blond wig completed my personage.

With the thought of Jean Louis Barrault's character in the film *The Children of Paradise* in my head, I meandered my unwordly self through the performance, complete with heavy feet and an expression of endless melancholy on my face. So far, so good.

However, one winter night, just before my entrance on the stage for the love duet with the soprano singing the role of Clarissa, the devil played a shabby trick on me. I had just paid a quick visit to the make-up room for a touchup of the giant teardrop that was marked under my left eye. The stage manager had already called my name over the dressing room loudspeaker. So, when the last "urgent" message came, I knew that I had but little time left to get ready for my first song on stage.

Like a battering ram, I tore out of the make-up room

en route to the steel stage door, sliding on my ballet slippers required by the role. Suddenly, I encountered a small puddle of water that was not supposed to be there and which I didn't see. As the German poet Heinrich Heine once wrote, "Also small things can be delightful."

Concentrating on taking the curve, I leaned heavily to starboard, like a sailing ship in full action, putting all my weight on one leg. As luck would have it, I stepped directly into the puddle, slipped as if on a banana peel, and landed on a metal table that also had no business being in the hallway.

The whole situation would have been a fine circus stunt, had it not been for the fact that I fell, full force, on my heart side against the sharply pointed iron corner of the table. The needle-like corner punctured the white satin costume, cracking two ribs, that in turn started pressing against my heart. Three seconds later, I lay kissing the marble floor of the corridor, gasping for a final gulp of oxygen.

The ingratiating soprano, alone on the stage, had long since reached the point of no return. Having been out of commission, so to speak, she recognized that she had no prospects of singing a duet by herself. Some members of the orchestra continued to hold the note of the last tone, hoping that I would make a last-minute entrance. The conductor stared at the stage in despair, where in all majesty, the curtain was being lowered.

Just about that time, the stage manager stepped in front of the footlights with the vigorous inquiry: "Is there a doctor in the house?"

"Yes Sir, over here," came an ominous voice from the audience.

"Will you please come backstage?" said the stage manager, invitingly, as if the doctor could expect the Nobel Prize for medicine.

In the meantime, I was carefully placed on the couch in my dressing room by cautious colleagues, and slowly regained consciousness. After the medicine man arrived,

Despite my agony, the show went on

he started undressing me, while getting an eyewitness report from a stagehand who had observed my stunt.

Exhaling caused me much pain, but when I tried to inhale the necessary air for survival, the torment was enough to make suffocation preferable. The doctor drew forth an injection syringe that seemed large enough to kill an elephant and, while giving me a shot in the arm, told the theater officials, "Go and inform the audience, the tenor will not be able to perform for the next three weeks."

Fortunately, at that moment, I was sufficiently recovered to perceive the threat by the *locum tenens* and gestured him to put his ear close to my mouth, like the touching scene of a soldier dying in Tolstoy's *War and Peace*. In a low whisper, I told the pill-roller that the night express to Vienna was waiting to take me at midnight to that city on the Danube River, where I was to make a new record album the next day, with the crew of the American Westminster label.

The conductor who had secured himself a position in the front row of those interested in the continuation of the performance, had also listened to my whisper campaign with the doctor. "If you can sing in Vienna tomorrow, you surely can continue singing here tonight," he said, opening a heated discussion, and with that, left in a huff.

Using his curative skills, the physician wrapped a stretch bandage around my chest, making sure that the loose ribs inside wouldn't rattle too much.

"But I still can't breathe," I whispered with a tear of pain in my voice, hoping to rouse the man's pity.

But as if his perceptive faculties had been eliminated, he declared mercilessly, "I will give you a shot of morphine that will freeze the pain and open the road to Vienna for you."

To sing or not to sing, that was the question!

Having been informed that the audience was still waiting, in its materialistic, egotistical "I want my money's worth" attitude, for the show to go on, I decided intrepidly that the show *would* go on at any cost. Walking like a kind of pseudo hunchback of Notre Dame, with my white face and painted teardrop on my cheek, I was almost the equivalent of the dotty Pierrot that I had to impersonate.

After the performance, I was celebrated like the Greek hero Odysseus after he had put an end to the 10-year siege of Troy by using a wooden horse. Because of my accident, the performance had taken a half-an-hour longer than usual. Consequently, I hardly had time to change into my street attire or to remove the make-up from my face if I wanted to be able to catch the midnight express to Vienna.

Although the morphine still had its anesthetizing effect, my fatigued appearance and disorderly face caused the sleeping car attendant to ask me if I needed a doctor.

"No Sir," I said, "I need a bed, and quickly!"

After having taken a double dose of a sedative, I climbed into my designated berth, still dressed in my travel clothes, and slept the sleep of the ignorant, unbeknownst to me that Damocles had already put his sword in place over my head.

At 5:30 the next morning, banging on my cabin door woke me up, accompanied with the message that we had arrived at Vienna's Train Terminal West. That was music to my ears.

Still dazed by the narcotics in my system, I cheerfully began to scramble to my feet. At that moment, without any warning, a pain shot through my carcass so vehemently that even a falcon would have grimaced with aversion. All the medicinal heartening-up, pills, injections and strong coffee had lost their effect as the passive voice of suffering once again took hold of me. When the train conductor observed my struggles, he again told me that a doctor or even a priest might be more suitable to the situation than a redcap.

I quickly made up a cock and bull story about being a doctor myself, and the good man even helped me by carrying my suitcase to the platform. Lonesome, but not alone, I waited until the train and the early birds had left the plat-

Despite my agony, the show went on

form before I made my first cautious steps in the direction of the microphones for the Westminster Recording Company.

Seeing an oversized baggage cart, I knew that the problem of moving my suitcase was solved. When I neared the end of the platform, a sign caught my eye: "Left Luggage Room." I told the man in charge that he could put my portmanteau on the luggage rack and should I kick the bucket, the suitcase would be his.

In the meantime, all the drugs in my body had lost their powers and the pain reached such a degree that I could not think normally anymore. Instead of taking a taxi, I started to walk through the still-dark streets of sleepy Vienna without really knowing where I was going.

The snow flurries that flew in my feverish face and the muddy slush that made walking even more arduous, didn't seem to bother me. It was a welcome relief to the high fever pounding in my deadly tired head. Halfway down the four-mile-long Mariahilferstrasse that eventually leads to the center of the town, a car with the word *Polizei* on the door, stopped beside me.

"What's up, fellow?" asked the patrolman through the window.

I stopped my random sauntering but could not have cared less about the cop, since he could not ease my pain one way or the other.

He got out of his patrol car and was just at the point of pushing me in the direction of his automobile when I started to explain in fits and starts about the opera singer who had just had an opera performance in Germany and was going to record for the American recording company Westminster at 10 o'clock that very morning with the Vienna Philharmonic Orchestra no less . . . etc.

"A fascinating story," remarked the constable, looking at his colleague. With a distrusting sneer on his civil servant visage, the other cop commented from the comfort of his car, "Let's face the music, but first, let's get him into the car. It's starting to get cold."

When I finally settled in behind the two lawmen, in the snug warmth of their home-away-from-home, they asked me how much and where had I been drinking until 6 a.m. in the morning. I shook my head wearily but there was no way I could convince them of my story.

"Let's get him to the hospital," they concluded and so, 30 minutes later, I was telling a doctor and his gentle nurse that same old story about the opera singer and the night before. As a *corpus delicti*, I was able to show the stretch bandage around my chest and so finally I developed some credibility with the doctor, which immediately resulted in another shot of something in my left arm. Then they wheeled me into a quiet room and several minutes later, I was sound asleep.

Around 11 a.m., I awoke with the subconscious suspicion that I actually should be recording an album at that moment and that the recording crew had already arrived from the United States and that they had no idea of their tenor's whereabouts.

"Stay where you are," said the kind nurse. "I will get the doctor."

After she had left the room, I picked up the telephone next to my bed, and with some difficulty, finally reached the production manager at Westminster.

"We're coming for you," said the irritated voice of the producer at the other end of the line, and 30 minutes later several members of Westminster, plus the conductor, Herman Scherchen, appeared at my bedside.

Hundreds of "whys" and "wherefores" were disseminated over my splitting head, again bursting with pain, but I could not provide a plausible explanation for my deportment.

"Doctor, this man *has* to sing today, cost what it may," said the producer, totally disregarding my condition. His attitude completely overthrew everything the musician's union considered justifiable and for which Equity has been striving since 1913.

"My advice is to wait one or two days" insisted the

Despite my agony, the show went on

negotiating physician.

"That will be $25,000 at the expense of this tenor," declared a highly emotional producer, as if he was auctioning me off at Sotheby's.

Shooting an additional dose of morphine into my exhausted body, the medicine man closed the conversation with the crabby statement, "Music is a sublime art."

One hour later I was placed in front of a microphone trying to accomplish an artwork of which posterity could one day say that it was, indeed, a work of art. For me, it was more or less a mission completed by hook and crook, but because the doctor had insisted that he would stay by my side during the entire recording session, keeping his amulet over my head as long as I could give vocal tones, the assignment was completed in time.

Westminster had its recording although the calculation of the expenses limped somewhat as a result of the doctor's bill. The work which we had recorded was Franz Joseph Haydn's *Seven Last Words of Christ*, and when I now listen to the recording, I cannot hide the thought that they also could have been my last words.

On the fourth day, I was finally able to fly home to Munich, where the nursing care of my forbearing wife, Louise, during my six weeks of residence between the sheets, easily let me forget the foolishness of my actions.

Several times again in my career, I handled such trifles as this one and every time I admonished my other self "If you ever repeat that stunt, I won't speak to you again!"

I wonder how many times I shall have to tell me that?!

Chapter Thirty

Shortcuts don't pay

During the late '50s, I was invited for the first time to sing at the world-famous Salzburg Music Festival. This is an honor that only two percent of the world's professional singers can ever dream of, let alone be asked back over a period of 18 seasons, as I had the privilege of being asked.

A conductor by the name of Meinhard von Zallinger, with whom I had studied opera-repertoire in Salzburg's Mozarteum music school, had not only an aristocratic family tree, but also two noble and dazzling young daughters whose well-shaped figures could hardly escape a man's attention. Both dolls did their utmost to let me share some fruits of their precociousness.

For a while, this pleasant pastime continued in a casual form, but when disagreement arose between the two as to who should have first choice, Mr. von Zallinger considered it advisable to take action. To get me as far away and as fast as possible from his progenies, he contrived a battle plan that would eventually change the direction of my life.

von Zallinger was, during those years, music director and first principal conductor of the *Komische Oper* (Light Opera House) in East Berlin which, at that time, was not disgraced by a dividing wall that obstructed one's vision, and where the communist dogma of the Stalin era had been proclaimed to "save the soul" of the working class.

The general manager of the *Komische Oper* was none other than the world-renowned stage director and theater personality, Austrian-born Walter Felsenstein. Conductor von Zallinger told "His Eminence" Felsenstein that he had heard a tenor in Salzburg who was good enough to have him "exiled" to East Berlin.

Consequently, three weeks later, I arrived in the metropolis on the Spree River, known at that time as the "Capital of the DDR (*Deutsche Demokratische Republik — German Democratic Republic*)."

I met the theater demigod Felsenstein in the midst of a stage rehearsal. The famous director observed me from beneath his thick eyebrows. His very blue Sinatra eyes became so penetrating as he looked me over that I feared they would pop out at any moment.

He asked me to sing an aria, which I dutifully proceeded to do. After three minutes, the audition was unceremoniously stopped. Was I to have traveled a thousand miles, crossing state and national boundary lines, for an audition of three minutes?

While I was struggling to give my artistic ego some dignity and myself my money's worth, a stagehand summoned by Felsenstein swept me gently, like an old broom, into a corner of the huge stage with the remark that my audition had indeed, been terminated. I packed my sheet music and walked, disillusioned, out of the theater and to my hotel.

Awaiting me there was a letter that had been delivered by a special courier from Walter Felsenstein. The message asked if I could take the delight in chaperoning Mrs. Felsenstein to the theater that same evening.

I had never met Maria Felsenstein but knew that she had previously been married to Germany's No. 1 film comedian, Paul Kemp, a man as popular in Germany at that time as Bob Hope is in the USA.

At the pre-concert hour, I called for Maria at the opera office, and together we crossed the Friedrichstrasse bridge to the Schiffbauerdamm Theater, where Bertolt Brecht's *The Caucasian Chalk Circle* was to be played that night.

This German playwright and poet who left his mark on contemporary historical expressionism, was the leader of the theatrical drama movement during the fifties.

Although the performance of the *Chalk Circle* that we saw that evening was of mediocre quality, I enjoyed the opportunity of hearing the famous dialogue. And when Maria promised to introduce me to Brecht at the lyricist's birthday celebration following the performance, my evening was made. I would be shaking the hand of the genial giant who had written the *Three Penny Opera*, *Galileo* and *Mother Courage*.

Dreams are deceptive! A short, skittish man with a too-small pair of nickel spectacles on his Pinocchio-like nose and a too-short, concentration camp coiffure, stood in front of me and ruined the mistaken notion that my imagination had created.

Maria, in the meantime, had poured several alcoholic beverages down her willing throat, mindful of the centuries-old maxim, "The spirit is willing, but the flesh is weak." Hanging her arms like eager tentacles around my neck, the gleam of alcoholic superabundance soon adorned her beautifully veiled eyes.

If eyes are indeed the mirror of the soul, it was a child's play to decipher the writing on the wall. Thus, under the influence, stories were committed to my ears that would have made even Casanova blush.

I also learned later that the letter, inviting me to the theater, that was given to me in the hotel lobby — presumably from Maria's husband, Walter — had been written by Maria herself.

With intimate, confidential boldness, she disclosed that in the recent past, the marriage vows between Walter and herself had been modified to "for worse and worse" and that I could be the one to have a more pleasing future. Sitting down, she placed both gloved hands far above where my knees had come to a stop.

Although Maria looked very appetizing in every respect with her lethargic Marlene Dietrich glance, she could have passed for my mother, rather than the girl next door.

Abruptly, I terminated the only time that she ever invited me to a theater performance, but her vengeance afterward was as remarkable as was her lust for love.

With the craftiness of a witch, Maria spread the rumor around the theater that I must be a homosexual. When sometime later, her husband, Walter, offered me the role of the young hero Tamino in Mozart's *The Magic Flute*, an unpleasant exchange ensued.

At his wife's instigation, Felsenstein ordered me to appear in his office and asked me delicately, "Are you a homosexual?"

Reacting like a provoked bull, I answered him in return with the question, "Are you a communist?"

After a silence that seemed to be an eternity, he replied with admirable frankness, but with a defiantly piercing tone, "No, I am not a member of the Communist Party."

"Well and I am not queer!" I declared with a trace of solemnity.

"My wife had reservations after your encounter with her at the theater and only a "straight" man can portray the role of Tamino in my stage production," said Felsenstein's, revealing the source of his inquiry.

I suggested that if he wished, I could give him a list of telephone numbers with names of the fair sex that would guarantee my genuine male composition.

He believed me and I went on to sing the role of Tamino some 45 times, much to the displeasure of Maria, who never spoke a single word to me again throughout my tenure at the opera house.

Two years after the incident, she exchanged her Walter for a mealy young tenor, who evidently was willing to put up with her marital escapades to further his singing career. How long her predatory power worked on him is not known by me, but his vocal cords were slackened before his promising career could take off.

Taking short-cuts in the theater doesn't *always* pay.

Chapter Thirty-One

From chaos to man

> We are the music makers,
> We are the dreamers of dreams,
> Wondering by lone sea-breakers,
> And sitting by desolate streams;
> World-losers and world forsakers,
> On whom the pale Moon gleams:
> We are the movers and the shakers
> Of the world forever, it seems.
>
> Arthur W. E. O'Shaughnessy
> (1844-1881)

As they flew, the ploughman stopped his work to gaze, and the shepherd leaned on his staff and watched the Moon, astonished at the notion that it was about to be visited by men and thinking, it must be gods who could leap from one celestial body to another.

On July 20, 1969, the utopical Icarus dream of humanity finally became reality. With a footstep and a flag, a 24-billion dollar American dream reached fulfillment. Some 3,000 days earlier, President John F. Kennedy had declared that the United States would put men on the Moon and bring them back safely to Earth before the decade was out and, Holy Mackerel, it was done.

After eight years of striving and seven astronauts' lives, with the labor of 60,000 managers and 400,000 technicians, a man from planet Earth stepped out of a landing craft, climbed down a few rungs of a ladder and put his feet on the dry and dusty lunar surface, 238,850 miles from his home in Ohio, proclaiming that it was "One small step for a man and... ugh... one giant leap for mankind." Subsequently he brought home moonbeams in a jar.

Now, I don't want to minimize the significance of this triumph in any way, but Neil Armstrong, Michael Collins and Buzz Aldrin were not the only people on Earth who made the globe go 'round that day. By no means!

It so happened that I looked after our good Mother Earth by having a performance that night of *The Merry Widow* at the *Theater an der Wien* in Vienna, and that is something not to be sneezed at. Most of the people whom I had spoken to that day were excited and with a healthy dash of imagination, I fancied myself to be the reason for their thrill. One must consider, though, that there may have been another reason for the excitement. The fact that the 4.6 billion-year-old Moon was about to be conquered by men, endowed with unquenchable thirst for knowledge, could not overlooked.

Everyone thinks his own geese are swans!

I had taken a small TV set with me to the theatre that night and plugged it in in my dressing room. Although my shuttling back and forth between the stage and my dressing room caused me to miss several crucial moments, I must credit Divine Providence for the privilege to join the celebration when Neil and Buzz set foot on lunar soil.

Personally, I would have preferred if some of that 24-billion dollar moon-money had been used to provide a 20-year supply of free powdered milk to starving African countries, but who am I to place hurdles before the evolution of mankind?

Since I was the only one who had brought a TV set to the theatre that night, the events on the Moon were my private knowledge. I let my enthusiasm take it course and called the manager of the theatre who had gone to his office to take a nap. I was quite emotional when I told him about the great gift that had just been handed to humanity

From chaos to man

and he, too, was ready to jump with joy.

Summer being a culturally slow season in Vienna, performances in that particular theatre (where at one time, long ago, the great Mozart yielded the scepter) are extremely popular and visitors from all over the world came to see the productions every year.

"In how many languages can you make this news known to the audience?" — the manager wanted to know. I told him that I could even tell naughty jokes in several European dialects.

"Just keep it clean and to the point," was his now somewhat uneasy answer. "Stop the performance and take the floor!"

I gratefully accepted the unique opportunity to become the first person in 200 years to freeze a performance in that legendary opera house. To put myself more clearly in the picture, I stopped the show at the most inconvenient moment, which made the conductor — who had no advance warning — become visibly older.

When the hall had finally turned dead silent and even the usually unflappable orchestra members stood up from their seats so as not to miss anything on stage, I placed myself like a statue in the spotlight intended for the soprano. In clear, theatrically articulate voice I delivered to my fellow earthlings the news of what has just taken place on our heavenly companion which faithfully follows us on our orbit around the Sun.

In four languages, I told the audience why I had broken the old rule that "The show must go on." Each time I had let the cat out of the bag in a given language, I received a standing ovation. And where even the greatest singers had never had a fourfold applause for the same aria in an opera, I enjoyed with deep gratitude this unique situation.

My final announcement was in English and I observed with great delight that a good number of American operetta enthusiasts were scattered here and there around the hall. Some started to cheer when I finished, but most of them silently rose on their feet, placed their right hand on their chest and began singing the American National Anthem at the top of their voices.

That this would turn out to be a risky enterprise in such a venerable temple of the muses would soon become the subject of discussion. Unfortunately, the courageous man who started this patriotic musical contribution had set it much too high. Without doubt, he had honorable intentions but he and his fellow singers inevitably went down a harmonic waterfall. When they arrived at "and the rockets' red glare," they could not climb that cliff and none of the loyal citizens was able to sing in pitch any more.

To show their American friends that Austrians sometimes can be helpful if it concerns a musical dilemma, several members of the neutral orchestra tried to remember the melody of the *Star-spangled Banner* and attempted to give some instrumental support. Soon, however, it became obvious that "Where there is a will, there is a way" would not do to keep with the solemnity of the occasion. Before long, the ensuing hilarity far exceeded the success of the operetta that night.

When the last tone of "and the home of the brave" had faded away, the atmosphere in the theatre was filled with great joy and goodwill to all people. It took a long time before the conductor and the soprano were able to resume *Vilia's Song* which had been so brusquely interrupted. And it sounded tedious and uninspired that night, following on the heels of the greatest event of the century.

At the end of the performance I enjoyed much more applause than any of my colleagues, thanks to three intrepid men. As far as I am concerned, they may go to the Moon as often as they want to, as long as I can be the singer who announces the great event during the performance.

Chapter Thirty-Two

I couldn't stop thinking about that lovely girl in blue

While studying at Salzburg's Mozarteum, I was offered my first singing engagement at the famous Music Festival of that historic city.

For a fledgling concert artist, it was often uncomfortable to be sitting on a stage where hundreds of eyes are riveted on your person. Involuntarily returning the stare of those eyes, the singer develops an extremely sensitive power of observation, where virtually nothing eludes his attention.

Every now and then, one encounters whispering and giggling which sometimes creates the insecure feeling in a male artist, making him nervously think: "Did I perhaps forget to zip up?" It takes a lot of willpower not to stand up and turn around while unobtrusively seeking the answer with one's fingertips. Since those first years, I have taken the trouble to have my tails and tux trousers tailored without openings for the necessities of life!

At that first concert engagement, I was inspecting the esteemed audience when my gaze fell upon a lovely creature in the fourth row, who commanded my undivided attention. She was dressed in a light blue two-piece coat dress with a pelerine. To be able to continue gazing unabashedly, I started blowing my nose whilst hiding behind my 12-inch handkerchief.

During the concert, I struggled to hold my music score at such an angle as to keep me from seeing the blue in the fourth row and the lovable smile that threatened my concentration.

The next day, I was driving across the old State Bridge

to the new section of Salzburg, when I suddenly saw the most beautiful blue of my life coming toward me from the opposite side of the bridge. It was now or never, I thought, and unheeding the solid yellow line separating the traffic, I made a swift U-turn as if driving a "dodge'em" car at Coney Island's Amusement Park.

Although I pushed the accelerator to the floor as if to ascend a 20 percent incline, reluctantly I had to realize that my prey had escaped down one of the narrow one-way lanes. A policeman, who had witnessed my reckless U-turn across the yellow line, had no appreciation of feminine esthetics and promptly fined me the equivalent of two New York strip steaks. But who cares about the consequences when beauty fires the blood and love exalts the mind!

The week after this frustrating event, I had a dinner engagement with a well-known American opera singer. I picked her up at her hotel by car and as we drove across the familiar Old Market Square, I casually glanced up at the second floor balcony of the legendary Café Tomaselli that has been selling coffee and pastries to Salzburgers and visitors from all over the world since 1792.

As if struck by lightening, I jumped up from behind my wheel the moment I detected the lovely countenance of the lady in blue. At the same instant, I was suddenly overcome by a very real distress in the abdomen of my lovesick body.

The soprano on my right diagnosed my Molierian account of distress immediately as appendicitis. I thanked her profusely for recognizing my intestinal inconvenience and swiftly as an arrow, I delivered her back to where I had picked her up half-an-hour earlier.

With undiminished celerity and burning with anticipation fueled by high hopes, I rushed back to Tomasellis to pay my respects to the girl from the fourth row. Meanwhile, a shoestring drizzle of rain, like a lace filigree, had began falling in the windless Salzburg night.

As I arrived at the place of no return, the fluttering of my cardiac valve was clearly audible. To my utmost con-

I couldn't stop thinking...

sternation, however, all I saw were lonely, empty chairs with shiny wet seats. I ran up the winding staircase to the abandoned terrace and entered the room where refreshments were being served. An ardent sigh of relief escaped my innermost soul as I saw the girl who was making me behave like a fourth grader.

Filled with unrestrained bliss, I jaunted up to the table where SHE was sitting. I was completely oblivious of the triviality that another fellow was sitting at the same table and talking so persuasively to her as if he was selling her a kingdom of goblins. Staring at my rival who, in a desperate struggle, was grasping her begloved hand so tightly as if he intended to keep it, I maneuvered myself into an undeserved predicament.

However, since a thing of beauty is a joy forever, I presented a defiant front to my competitor by asking in a nonchalant tone of voice if the third chair at the table was still available. Intimidated by my bold liberties, the offended man looked at me as though he had seen Jerry Falwell waving the hammer and sickle banner.

Since in Europe it is quite acceptable to join other diners at a table when there is place, he said, civilly, "Sit wherever you like. All the chairs are free to be used," pointing to 25 empty chairs and tables.

"Thank you," I said with pseudo politeness, "then I will sit here." And with that, I sat down at their table.

My presence was as superfluous as counting box cars at a railroad junction. After I had gone through 20 minutes of unbearable emotional strain, the man finally dropped the gloved hand, stood up and left the room.

They had not said one more word since my arrival. I surmised that he had gone where even kings and queens have to go alone, but that assumption was just a lover's apprehension, as he never did return.

Looking at the lonesome beauty, I detected behind the tears of unhappiness a gleam of blithesome sunrise and a sense of freedom, all the while looking at me with a cheerful smile that totally eclipsed Mona Lisa's famous smirk. I felt the time was ripe to take the bull by the horns.

I proceeded to tell her that I had seen her at my concert sitting in the fourth row, wearing a blue dress with a bolero. Also that I had seen her one day just as she was crossing the main bridge, but that she had unfortunately disappeared down a narrow street.

Clumsy and stuttering, I had to realize that my German monologue was hanging in the air inextricable to the ear of my listener who was hanging on my very lips.

"English?" I asked, since it was becoming clear that my words might have been in Chinese, as far as she was concerned. "Yes," came the soft answer with a sigh of relief, "American."

I continued to rattle on and on, as if my life depended on it. My mastery of the English language was fortunately decent enough to tell my table partner that I was hungry and that dinner for two in a small, candle-lit inn would be the right beginning for a cozy evening.

When the sun had long pushed itself away from the horizon of the new morning and with the milkman already on his way home, Louise and I exchanged the first attributes for a long-lasting homogeneity.

That love and marriage go together like a horse and carriage was verified five months later as we drove together to the Old Town Hall in The Hague in Holland, the first in a long line of carriages drawn by white horses with red-plumed headgear and coachmen in livery. I have been grateful ever since that I looked up to that terrace on that drizzling, rainy night in that old town of Salzburg, for since that time, Louise and I have been married for over 30 years.

Therefore, I offer this advice to all love-hungry bachelors: go to that special Austrian music village of Salzburg and take one of the many horsedrawn carriages that pass Café Tomaselli. But don't forget to look up to the terrace in joyful anticipation!

Chapter Thirty-Three

An emotional decision

The year was 1978. Louise and I were still living in Munich, the capital city of Bavaria, nestled at the foot of the German Alps. Postwar Munich had been rebuilt from total destruction into a lovely modern city of a million, a society of beer and *lederhosen*.

One-hundred miles to the northeast of Munich was the then heavily-guarded border of then Czechoslovakia where communists were still offering their countrymen and women the same ideological promises that a certain Ulianov, better known as Vladimir Lenin had shouted in 1917 from the city walls of Tsarist St. Petersburg.

At that time, my singing schedule consisted of up to 300 performances a year on all the continents of the globe. I deeply yearned for a year of sleep and then to retire to a five-acre horse ranch, read Steinbeck and Goethe, and sit in a rocking chair in front of a crackling fire on a crisp autumn evening.

One dreary day, during our morning coffee break, I revealed those sentiments to Louise, my always understanding wife.

"Do you want to begin a new career as a singing farmer? — was her initial reaction.

"No, I want to stop singing, PERIOD!" — I said and was surprised to hear that coming out of my mouth.

Louise put her coffee cup slowly down on the table beside her. After a long, pregnant silence, she looked up at me in that certain way she has when she knows that her answer is of momentous importance.

"But your music is your life. You can't live without it

and, besides, your family and fans would never forgive you!"

I had to admit that that aspect had never crossed my mind.

I was never easily daunted, so I grumbled that there were perhaps a million other tenors in the world to whom my fans could switch their allegiance.

Louise easily broke through my defense with the simple statement that those tenors had other names and that she thought that there was only one ME.

With that final remark, she hung the battle ax on the coat rack.

Many months went by while I continued to sing for my supper but the thoughts of a pending monumental decision made me more restless than ever before. In my subconscience I knew that I was in contact with something that I could not define; nevertheless, it was there, waiting to be dealt with.

In 1975, the Bavarian government honored me with the title *Kammersänger* (Court Singer) and because of this distinction, I often met on social occasions with Bavarian state officials, with whom I talked, when at all possible, about my second favorite subject — politics.

The world situation looked rather gloomy in those years and no one could foresee the near future; no one knew how far the ideology-driven expansion of communism would go. Many German Jews had been too optimistic in 1933 when Hitler came to power. They paid with their lives for remaining in the evil empire of Nazism.

Then there was party boss Leonid Brezhnev of the then U.S.S.R., who was an incalculable and inscrutable contemporary. The reconciliation kiss that was bestowed on him by a well-meaning but naive President Jimmy Carter, was looked upon as a political prostration by the leaders of Europe.

The week following that unnatural embrace, I put my house in Munich up for sale. This raised a three-dimen-

An emotional decision

sional dilemma:

1. I still had an active singing career.
2. Our many friends were opposed to our departure.
3. Where to go?

The fact that I am Dutch and Louise an American, made it somewhat easier to convince friends and colleagues that in the eyes of the Bavarian state, we were temporary residents, or legal aliens at best, who had been "employed guests" in Germany for 24 years.

I felt a restless urge to move to a far-away land of liberty, with another culture, another climate, language, atmosphere and people. The Dutch say of themselves that being Dutch is not only a nationality but also a state of mind. This characteristic makes it less troublesome to live in another civilized tradition.

New Zealand was high on our list but an American composer friend who lived in Hollywood, California, before moving to New Zealand, assured us that that gorgeous country down under was undoubtedly very far away for a composer, but thanks to fax and phone, the distance was not insurmountable. However, we were reminded, an opera singer still had to carry his tools in his throat, and travel.

Some weeks later, Providence was on our side, as I was invited, for the first time, to sing in Miami, half-a-world away from Munich where we still lived. Since this was my very first Florida experience, everything was new to me.

At the invitation of an old friend who lived in North Palm Beach, I was picked up in Miami and chauffeured around Palm Beach County like a head of state. For the first time since my marriage 22 years before, I fell in love again! This was it!

That night I called my wife in Munich, persuading her to take the next plane for Florida so that I could introduce her to the Lady who had stolen my heart: Palm Beach County.

The second day after Louise's arrival, Hurricane David sent us scurrying north, to save our souls (and bodies) from torrential destruction. Lady Florida had shown us her claws, as if to test our affection.

When we returned from three days in Orlando, the ever-inviting sunshine was her innocent old self again, as if nothing had happened at all. We tossed a coin and settled down in Tequesta, the lovely bedroom community straddling the border between Palm Beach and Martin counties.

Our Munich home was sold in two days so that the United States of America might welcome two brand new residents.

Having promised myself never to sing one single tone of music anymore after leaving Munich and the theatre world, the first two Florida years were a Robinson Crusoe adventure, thanks to the unchallenged isolation of the completely new development in Tequesta where we had decided to live.

After those years of idleness and enjoyment, however, the cup of the land of plenty was brimming over. Eventually, we discovered that Florida was not only coastline but that it even had a large lake in its center with a, for us, unpronounceable name.

After someone instructed us how to pronounce Okeechobee, we drove to the lake to admire the lush landscaping and glorious villas we had expected to find on the lakefront. To our disillusionment, however, we only saw poverty and misery among the often desperate residents.

After returning home that day, we found ourselves in a mental turmoil and decided to do something to alleviate at least the hunger of those most vulnerable. That night, we founded the food relief organization, Help the Hungry at Home, Inc., which, up to this day, has fed thousands of indigent people.

To create the financial backing for such an enterprise, we founded the Blowing Rocks Music Festival which not only brings orchestras and choruses, famous conductors and soloists to our area annually, but also made me dust-off my retired vocal cords again so they could be used to "sing for someone else's supper."

Our motto became, "We turn music into food." It is our wish that this will go on for many more years, and that we may pass our days here, where we found support and friends.

"Nothing is worth more than this day." (Johann Wolfgang von Goethe, 1786)

Chapter Thirty-Four

It's a tough life

It is by no means meant to sound arrogant or disrespectful when in the last chapter of this book I would like to draw a comparison between the professional struggles of instrumentalists and vocalists.

For a violinist, it is apparently less constraining with his four-stringed instrument to shape a life-long career out of his own aspirations. Why great violinists like Oistrach or Paganini stopped concertizing midway their brilliant careers, only the good Lord knows, but His ways are mysterious, as is generally known.

In contrast to vocalists, instrumentalists have the unfair advantage of being able to depend on technology for assistance — something not available to singers. As long as ebony, maple or fir will grow, composers will write creations for string instruments.

If the string of a violin snaps, the performer can keep on playing with the remaining three strings until he has a moment to lay a new string on his instrument, without interrupting the concert. If, what is often the case, he gets tired of the occasionally poor sound of his mediocre fiddle, he can always go to the bank and borrow enough money to buy a valuable Guernieri or even a Stradivarius.

With the same four fingers that produced only a diminutive sound with the previous stringbox, he now creates superbly warm tones from his precious new wonderbox. Suddenly, he is a new superstar who is much in demand. It is all a matter of money, not artistry.

Pianists have their instrument tuned if their tin kettle sounds as if it had ice cubes under its hood. After the tuning, the piano-on-the-rocks can render another year of joyful noise at weddings and parties.

An organist can have a trained expert look at his pipes if they sound more like a factory siren and restore their glorious resonance which has brought joy to countless cherubs decorating church organs all over the world.

A timpanist braces a new skin if he has exaggerated the fortissimo prescribed by the composer and has punched holes through the lining of his stew pot. The oboist can always take a new reed if the old one has been sucked to pieces.

What can we, pitiable vocalists do when after endless years of service, the vocal cords begin sounding more like elastic bands, rather than producing radiant tones. We can only hope that Providence has blessed us with longevity as far as our ability to make music is concerned.

Has anyone ever heard of a violinist, bassoonist, flutist or harpist sitting at least once a week in the examining chair of an otolaryngologist to have his uvula inspected to make sure that all is well on the vocal front? Has anyone ever seen a clarinetist, horn player or any other blow-happy instrumentalist go to the pharmacy every week in wintertime to purchase expensive pills or drops for an advancing cold, dried-out membranes, or a simple laryngitis?

No, a thousand times no! No other musician than a vocalist has to undergo all these tormenting ordeals to please their audiences. Yet, vocalists do not complain while suffering on the torture rack of the medicine man and making a considerable contribution to the elevated life style of that bone-crusher.

Yes, the singer bears the cross of his profession without a cry of distress and resigns to his fate whatever it may be. The vocalist is a *homo sapiens* with a tremendous sense of devotion to his fans, as well as his bank account. He is not ashamed to demand a higher concert fee than an instrumentalist, fully knowing that his singing days are numbered. He does not fritter away his hard-earned savings on unneeded instruments; he faithfully invests them instead at a local financial institution at the highest interest rate possible so that he may bolster the economy of his beloved fatherland. The vocalist does all of this without self-indulgence. He only hopes for a favorable obituary and that cultural posterity will be kind to him.

The reader will understand that I don't anticipate an early ending of my life experiences as far as my singing career is concerned. I want to remain true to my life-long motto: "Carry on your trade to the benefit of the community and amass earthly goods as long as they are given to you."

Amen!

About the author

Place of birth: The Hague, The Netherlands
Current residence: Palm Beach County, Florida
Nationality: Dutch
Education:
    Graduated with diploma in Electrical Engineering, The Hague School of Technology
    Five years of full scholarship, with ensuing diploma from The Royal Conservatory, The Hague
    Three years of private voice training in The Netherlands
    Three years of summer courses at the *Mozarteum*, Salzburg, Austria
    Two years of voice training with Vera Schwarz in Vienna, Austria and in New York
    One year *Harmony* and *Theory* with Nadia Boulanger in Paris
Concert Debut:
    Beethoven's *Ninth Symphony* in Zürich, Switzerland, Charles Mnnch conducting
Opera Debut:
    Richard Strauss' *Der Rosenkavalier* with the Vienna State Opera, Erich Kleiber conducting
Prizes:
    First Tenor Prize, *International Vocal Competition*, Geneva, Switzerland
    First Prize, *International Competition*, Brussels, Belgium
    Second Prize, *National Vocal Competition*, Scheveningen, The Netherlands

Awards:
- *The Golden Rose* music critics' prize, Munich, Germany
- *Man of Achievement* award, Cambridge University, England
- *Prix d'Italia* for motion picture performances of Mozart's *Le Nozze di Figaro* and Orff's *Carmina Burana*
- Elected member of *Accademia Italia delle Arte*, Florence, Italy
- VIP Encyclopedia Corporation, Delaware, *Certificate Award* for listing in all editions of *Who's Who in The World*
- *Congressional Award* presented to Sir John van Kesteren in recognition of the 10th anniversary of *Help the Hungry at Home*
- Television Award, *Operation T.N.T.*
- Awards for outstanding community service on behalf of of *Help the Hungry at Home:*
  - *Outstanding Community Award*, TV-12 West Palm Beach
  - Proclamation of the Town of Jupiter (twice)
  - Proclamation of the Village of Tequesta (twice)
  - Palm Beach County Board of Commissioners
  - Nomination for National *Jefferson Award* (twice)
  - National Head Start
  - *Golden Key Award* of JupiterTequesta Kiwanis

Honors:
- Title of *Kammersänger* from the German Government
- *Knight of Orange-Nassau*, conferred by Queen Juliana of The Netherlands
- Elevation to *Officer of the Royal House of Orange-Nassau* by Queen Beatrix of The Netherlands
- *Federal Cross of Merit with Ribbon*, conferred by the President of the Federal Republic of Germany
- Member of *Merit for Life, Confederation of Chivalry*, Australia

About the author

Member of Opera Houses:
  Berlin (East), five years
  Berlin (West), three years
  Munich, 20 years

Concert Performances:
  Throughout the world, with the exception of South Africa; including Paris, London, Edinburgh, Stockholm, Copenhagen, Amsterdam, Antwerp, Brussels, Barcelona, Madrid, Berlin, Munich, Vienna, Salzburg, Moscow, St. Petersburg, Warsaw, New York, Cincinnati, Buffalo, Dallas, Los Angeles, Palm Beach, Washington, Montreal, Winnipeg, Quebec, Ottawa, Vancouver, Calgary, Hong Kong, Bombay, as well as cities in Italy, Japan, Thailand, Australia, New Zealand, Indonesia, Argentina, Brazil, etc.

Television:
  Countless opera and operetta performances in Germany, Austria and The Netherlands
  Global television concert with the Berlin Philharmonic in commemoration of the dropping of the atom bomb on Hiroshima
  Televison performances in Indonesia marking the resumption of cultural ties between Indonesia and The Netherlands
  Own personality show with Mrs. van Kesteren on Dutch Television

Opera:
  Thirty years as guest artist in most of the major opera houses of the world, including *Deutsche Oper* in Berlin, Vienna, Munich, Amsterdam, Brussels, Hamburg, Zürich, Madrid, Barcelona, etc.

Festivals:
  Salzburg (12 times), Edinburgh (twice), Flanders (Antwerp), Munich (15 times), Berlin (seven times), La Scala (Milano), Vienna, Florence, Peruga, Rome, Madrid, Buenos Aires, Rio de Janeiro, Drottning-

holm, Herrenhausen, Schwetzingen, Ravinia (Chicago), Montreal (11 times), etc.

Royal Performances:
    UNICEF Gala for Queen Beatrix, The Hague
    Gala performance for Queen Elisabeth, Brussels
    Gala performance for King Juan Carlos and Queen Sophia, Madrid
    For Princess Christina of The Netherlands, Montreal

Specialty:
    Opera and concert classical repertoire, arts songs, operetta
    Has sung more than 500 performances of J. S. Bach's *Passion* in the capital cities of five continents with the leading orchestras of the world, under the baton of many renowned conductors, including Klemperer, Pritchard, Bernstein, Kleiber, Kubelik, von Karajan, Barenboim, Barbirolli, Böhm, Muti, Mehta, Frübeck, Leinsdorf, Richter, Decker, etc.

Recordings:
    Twenty-seven separate albums, including opera, operetta, concert and solo performances

Organizations:
    Founder and Artistic Director of the *Blowing Rocks Music Festival*, Jupiter, Florida
    Founder and President-General Manager of the food relief organization *Help the Hungry at Home, Inc.* in South Florida

Help The Hungry At Home

Mindful of the wretchedness of his youth during World War II when famine and enmity were the order of the day in his home country of The Netherlands and later, in the United States, seeing hunger and misery among indigent people in parts of South Florida, Sir John and Louise van Kesteren decided to try to help those who cannot help themselves.

In 1983 they founded the food relief organization, *Help the Hungry at Home, Inc.* in Tequesta, South Florida, which delivers food on a regular basis to people in need, regardless of race, religion or national background.

Under the motto, "We turn music into food," they launched in 1988 the annual *Blowing Rocks Music Festival* in Jupiter, Florida. With critically acclaimed, high-quality performances, the Festival raises funds for the food program.

Information about both programs may be obtained through P. O. Box 3851, Tequesta, Florida 33469

An audio cassette of *My Heart Is Full of Sunshine*, with John van Kesteren accompanied by the Vienna Philharmonic, is available at $5.00 per copy. Add $2.00 shipping/handling. $7.00 postpaid.

Send checks or money orders to . . .

> van Kesteren Audio Cassette
> P. O. Box 3851
> Tequesta, FL 33469-0851